If Not Stocks, What?

If Not Stocks, What?

Gene Walden

McGraw-Hill

NEW YORK   CHICAGO   SAN FRANCISCO
LISBON   LONDON   MADRID   MEXICO CITY
MILAN   NEW DELHI   SAN JUAN   SEOUL
SINGAPORE   SYDNEY   TORONTO

1 2 3 4 5 6 7 8 9 0   AGM/AGM   1 0 9 8 7 6 5 4 3

ISBN 0-07-142149-1

This publication is designed to provide accurate and authoritative information in regard to the subject matter covered. It is sold with the understanding that neither the author nor the publisher is engaged in rendering legal, accounting, or other professional service. If legal advice or other expert assistance is required, the services of a competent professional person should be sought.
> —*From a declaration of principles jointly adopted by a committee of the American Bar Association and a committee of publishers*

McGraw-Hill books are available at special quantity discounts to use as premiums and sales promotions, or for use in corporate training programs. For more information, please write to the Director of Special Sales, Professional Publishing, McGraw-Hill, Two Penn Plaza, New York, NY 10121-2298. Or contact your local bookstore.

Library of Congress Cataloging-in-Publication Data

Walden, Gene.
    If not stocks, what? / By Gene Walden.
      p. cm.
    ISBN 0-07-142149-1 (pbk. : alk. paper)
   1. Portfolio management—United States. 2. Investments—United States. 3. Bonds—United States. I. Title.
HG4529.5 .W354 2003
332.6—dc21
                                      2003012927

 This book is printed on recycled, acid-free paper containing a minimum of 50% recycled de-inked paper.

Contents

Acknowledgments

I WANT TO THANK the people who made this book possible, including Robert Fransen, who provided some very helpful insight into real estate investing, my editor, Stephen Isaacs, who helped shape the book, the editing supervisor, Sally Glover, and my literary agent, Carol Mann.

BEYOND STOCKS

MILLIONS OF AMERICAN investors have learned a very expensive lesson about stocks: They don't always go up.

Over the past few years, investors have lost about $6 trillion dollars in the stock market, the biggest single decline in dollar terms in stock market history. That amounts to about $20,000 for every man, woman, and child in America.

The problem for most investors who lost big—including the millions who saw their 401K plans, their IRAs, or their other investment or college savings accounts shrivel to a fraction of their peak value—is that they had little or no diversification beyond stocks.

In truth, there was little reason to buy anything else. Stocks were on such a furious run through the 1990s that their returns dwarfed everything else in sight. Why settle for a 7-percent bond when you could get 40 percent with a high-tech mutual fund? And why ever sell when stocks seemed to go up year after year almost without fail. Diversification beyond the stock market would have served only to slow down the runaway train.

But when the bear market struck, investors were caught unaware of how to invest in anything except stocks and stock mutual funds. Most 401K plans and other company retirement plans offered few if any options beyond the company stock or a few stock and bond mutual funds.

Bank accounts and short-term CDs offer virtually no return, and complex investments such as commodities and options are beyond the realm of possibility for most working Americans.

But there is a wide array of other investment choices out there, including some with very respectable returns. For long-term returns, stocks know no match, but by adding other ingredients to your portfolio, you can smooth out the rough ride and keep your investment portfolio growing steadily.

This book lays out the basics of more than 20 different types of investments that you could consider using to balance your portfolio. Some offer income; others come with the capital appreciation potential. Some can save you on your taxes; others provide a hedge against inflation. Remember, a well-balanced portfolio with the right combination of investments can keep you on the road to prosperity.

REITS (REAL ESTATE INVESTMENT TRUSTS)

High Income, Inflation Hedge

IF YOU OWN YOUR OWN HOME, then you have a stake in the real estate market. But the commercial real estate investment market moves in a different cycle than the housing market and can provide some benefits that home ownership doesn't. If you want a stake in the commercial real estate market, there is no easier way to invest than to buy shares of a real estate investment trust (REIT).

REITs are like stocks for the commercial real estate industry. They are trusts that buy commercial properties, such as apartments, office buildings, and shopping centers that produce income. When you buy shares of a REIT, you become a part owner in all of the property holdings of the REIT.

REITs are traded like stocks on the major stock exchanges, so they provide the liquidity of stocks with the diversification and income of commercial real estate.

REITs were first approved by Congress in 1960 to offer small investors a chance to participate in the commercial real estate market. Although they were slow to catch on initially, they have become increasingly popular in recent years. There are now more than 200 REITs available on the major stock exchanges, including about 150 REITs on the New York Stock Exchange, and dozens more on the American Stock Exchange and NAS-DAQ market. You can buy them through any broker and follow them in the daily stock listings of many newspapers (or the Internet).

REITs have several attractive features. They pay among the highest yields of all types of investments, the dividends often increase from year to year, and they are easy to buy, sell, and follow.

There are several different types of REITs available on the market:

- Equity REITs own and operate income-producing real estate, such as apartments, warehouses, office buildings, hotels, and shopping centers.

- Specialized REITs focus on a particular type of property, such as shopping centers or health care facilities.

- Geographically focused REITs specialize in a single region or metropolitan area, while others try to acquire properties throughout the country. Mortgage REITs lend money to real estate owners and operators and raise income from the interest payments on the mortgages.

- Hybrid REITs own properties and provide loans to real estate owners.

  REITs are closely regulated, and must meet certain requirements:

- Must be managed by a board of directors.

- Must pay shareholder dividends of at least 90 percent of its taxable income.

- Must invest at least 75 percent of total assets in real estate assets.

- Must derive at least 75 percent of gross income from rents from real property or interest on mortgages on real property.

- Must be managed by a board of directors.

- Must have a minimum of 100 shareholders.

- Must have no more than 50 percent of the shares held by five or fewer individuals.

WHO SHOULD BUY REITS?

REITs are geared to both large and small investors interested in current income and a stake in the real estate market as part of a diversified portfolio.

WHO SHOULD NOT BUY REITS?

REITs would not be attractive to investors looking for capital appreciation. REITs distribute 90 to 100 percent of pretax earnings each year to shareholders in the form of dividends, but the value of the shares tends to change very little from year to year.

REITs also may not be appropriate for you if you don't need the income and you want to minimize your taxes. The dividends paid by REITs are added to your total taxable income, so you will owe more taxes—unless you use REITs in your IRA or other tax-deferred retirement plan.

RETURN

The rate of return offered by REITs is outstanding as compared with other income-producing investments. In recent years, while money market funds were paying 1 to 2 percent and many government bonds were paying less than 5 percent, many REITs were paying dividends of 6 to 12 percent. And the dividends for many REITs increase nearly every year, providing yet another advantage over bonds and other traditional fixed-income investments.

RISKS

Although most REITs provide pretty steady performance, there are risks with REITs. In a down economy, if vacancies increase in the commercial properties owned by the REIT, income could decline. In a very slow market, you could see a decline in your income as well as in the value of your REIT shares.

UPSIDE

The biggest upside to REITs may be their high yields, but there are some other benefits as well, such as:

- **Increasing stream of income.** REITs often increase their dividends each year, providing investors with a steadily increasing stream of income.

- **Inflation hedge.** Owning real estate can be an inflation hedge. Real estate often rises in value along with inflation, so the value of your investment in real dollars stays about the same regardless of inflation. And the increasing stream of income that REITs provide compensates for the increasing costs of inflation.

- **Professional management.** Professional real estate managers run the business, select the properties, handle the maintenance and leasing and the many other intricate details of the business, while you sit home and collect your dividend checks.

- **Easy to buy.** Buying REITs is as easy as calling your broker or making a few clicks in your online brokerage account. REITs trade like stocks on the major stock exchanges, so they are very easy to buy and sell. They give you a chance to own real estate without evaluating properties, dealing with real estate agents and bankers, and personally maintaining the properties.

- **Low price of admission.** The cost of buying commercial real estate on your own could be millions of dollars. Even in a limited-partnership real estate deal, you might be required to put up $25,000 to $100,000 or more. But with REITs, you can pick your price. If you want to buy a few hundred dollars or a few thousand dollars worth of REIT shares, you have that option. In fact, you can buy shares of two or three REITs if you want to diversify within the REIT universe. It's all very affordable.

- **Liquidity.** You can buy or sell REITs whenever the stock market is in session, so you have excellent liquidity. By contrast, many limited partnerships require you to leave your money in for 5 to 10 years. Or if you own your own commercial property, selling it can be a major ordeal. With a REIT, you can buy or sell with a call to your broker or a couple of clicks in your online brokerage account.

DOWNSIDE

The downside to REITs is that they provide little, if any, capital appreciation. They do provide excellent income, but that income is taxable, so it can increase your tax burden (unless you use REITs in your IRA or other tax-deferred retirement plan).

HOW TO BUY REITS

Buying REITs is the same as buying stocks. You can buy shares of REITs through your broker or through any online broker.

BIGGEST CONCERNS

The value of your REIT shares and the dividend they pay depends on the strength of the real estate market. In a depressed real estate market, you could see the value of your shares decline. In a bad commercial real estate market, rising vacancy rates would also cut into income collected by the REIT, which would reduce the amount of your dividend.

TIMING

It would be a good idea to have a small portion of REITs in your portfolio at all times because of the diversification they offer. However, they are particularly attractive during periods of low interest rates and a down stock market. Typically when stocks are faltering, real estate can buoy the portfolio. And when bond interest rates are low, REITs can provide a much better stream of income.

REITs are less attractive when the stock market is booming—since returns from REITs fall short of the average annual returns from stocks. They are also less attractive during periods of high interest rates, when you can do almost as well with government bonds and triple A corporate bonds as you would with a REIT.

The perfect time to buy a REIT is when the economy is coming out of recession and business is picking up. At that point, real estate prices may still be a little depressed, but business growth will soon lead to higher office and warehouse occupancy rates.

MONITORING YOUR REITS

You can follow your REITs exactly as you follow any stock. REIT share prices are listed in the usual stock tables in the business section of many major newspapers: *USA Today*, *The Wall Street Journal*, or *Investor's Business Daily*. You can also find their current share prices on the Internet at any of the many financial Web sites that feature stock prices. Most REITs trade on the New York Stock Exchange, the American Stock Exchange, or the NASDAQ market, although some are traded on the smaller over-the-counter market.

ASSET ALLOCATION

As with all types of investments, the amount of your savings that you allocate for REITs should depend on your tax situation, your financial situation, your investment goals, and your tolerance for risk.

Investors interested in income might want to load up on REITs, with 10 to 30 percent of your portfolio in REITs, because they offer a stream of income that is among the best in the investment market.

Because they are taxable, unless you need the income, you might want to put your REITs in your tax-sheltered retirement account.

SPECIAL CONSIDERATIONS

When selecting a REIT, you may want to look at several factors:

- What is the dividend yield and how does that compare with other REITs? Because income is the main benefit of REITs, you may as well look for one that pays a relatively high return.

- What is its track record? Look at the REIT's past growth record and dividend payment history. Look for a REIT that has maintained a fairly steady stock price the past few years, and, perhaps even more importantly, a steadily increasing dividend.

- Check out the company. Nearly all REITs have a Web site. Go to the Web site, check out the information on the company, its history, its management, and its investment properties. You might want to look over several REITs to compare and contrast before making a decision. If the yield is high, the track record is solid with steadily rising dividends, and the company and its management look good, that's a good sign. However, for the sake of safety and diversification, you might want to spread your money around to two or three different REITs.

- How is the market for the type of properties the REIT owns? For instance, if office space or apartment units are filling up around the country, there's a good chance that REITs that invest in those types of properties would soon see an increase in earnings. But if the economy is slowing down and vacancies are rising, you may want to avoid those REITs.

Here is a list of the REITs that trade on the major stock exchanges:

NEW YORK STOCK EXCHANGE

Company Name	Ticker
Acadia Realty Trust	AKR
Agree Realty Corporation	ADC
Alexander's, Inc.	ALX
Alexandria Real Estate Equities, Inc.	ARE
AMB Property Corporation	AMB
America First Mortgage Investments, Inc.	MFA
American Land Lease	ANL
American Residential Investment Trust, Inc.	INV
Amli Residential Properties Trust	AML
Annaly Mortgage Management, Inc.	NLY
Anthracite Mortgage Capital, Inc.	AHR
AIMCO	AIV
Apex Mortgage Capital, Inc.	AXM
Archstone-Smith	ASN
Arden Realty Group, Inc.	ARI
Asset Investors Corporation	AIC
Associated Estates Realty Corp.	AEC
AvalonBay Communities, Inc.	AVB
Bedford Property Investors	BED
Boston Properties, Inc.	BXP
Boykin Lodging Company	BOY

Brandywine Realty Trust...BDN
Brookfield Properties Corporation ....BPO
BRE Properties, Inc. ....BRE
BRT Realty Trust...BRT
Burnham Pacific Properties, Inc. ....BPP
California Preferred Capital Corp. ....CFP
Camden Property Trust..CPT
Capstead Mortgage Corporation ....CMO
CarrAmerica Realty Corporation..CRE
Catellus Development Corporation..CDX
CBL & Associates Properties ....CBL
Center Trust Properties...CTA
CenterPoint Properties Trust..CNT
Chateau Communities, Inc. ....CPJ
Chelsea Property Group...CPG
Chevy Chase Preferred Capital Corp..CCP
Clarion Commercial Holdings, Inc..CLR
Colonial Properties Trust...CLP
Commercial Net Lease Realty ....NNN
Cornerstone Realty Income Trust ....TCR
Corporate Office Properties Trust...OFC
Correctional Properties Trust...CPV
Cousins Properties, Inc. ....CUZ
Crescent Real Estate Equities, Inc. ....CEI
CRIIMI MAE, Inc..CMM
Crown American Realty Trust ....CWN
Developers Diversified Realty Corporation...DDR
Duke Realty Corporation...DRE
EastGroup Properties, Inc. ....EGP
Elder Trust ....ETT
Entertainment Properties Trust..EPR
Equity Inns, Inc. ....ENN
Equity Office Properties Trust ....EOP
Equity One, Inc..EQY
Equity Residential...EQR
Essex Property Trust, Inc. ....ESS
Federal Realty Investment Trust ....FRT
FelCor Lodging Trust, Inc..FCH
First Industrial Realty Trust ....FR
First Union Real Estate Investments ....FUR

Forest City Enterprises ....FCE.A
Gables Residential Trust ....GBP
General Growth Properties, Inc. ....GGP
Glenborough Realty Trust, Inc. ....GLB
Glimcher Realty Trust...GRT
Great Lakes REIT..GL
Health Care Property Investors, Inc...HCP
Health Care REIT, Inc. ....HCN
Healthcare Realty Trust, Inc...HR
Highwoods Properties, Inc..HIW
Home Properties of New York, Inc. ....HME
Hospitality Properties Trust..HPT
Host Marriott Corporation ....HMT
HRPT Properties Trust..HRP
Innkeepers USA Trust ....KPA
IRT Property Company..IRT
iStar Financial, Inc. ....SFI
JDN Realty Corporation..JDN
Keystone Property Trust ....KTR
Kilroy Realty Corporation ....KRC
Kimco Realty Corporation...KIM
Koger Equity, Inc...KE
Konover Property Trust, Inc...KPT
Kramont Realty Trust..KRT
La Quinta Properties, Inc. ....LQI
LaSalle Hotel Properties..LHO
LASER Mortgage Management, Inc. ....LMM
Lexington Corporate Properties, Inc...LXP
Liberty Property Trust...LRY
LTC Properties, Inc...LTC
Macerich Company, The ....MAC
Mack-Cali Realty Corporation..CLI
Malan Realty Investors, Inc. ....MAL
Manufactured Home Communities ....MHC
MeriStar Hospitality Corporation..MHX
Mid-America Apartment Communities, Inc......................................MAA
Mid-Atlantic Realty Trust..MRR
Mills Corporation, The ....MLS
Montgomery CV Realty Group CVI
National Golf Properties, Inc. ....TEE

National Health Investors, Inc. ....NHI
Nationwide Health Properties, Inc...NHP
New Plan Excel Realty Trust..NXL
Novastar Financial, Inc..NFI
Omega Healthcare Investors, Inc...OHI
Origen Financial, Inc...OFI
Pacific Gulf Properties ....PAG
Pan Pacific Retail Properties..PNP
Parkway Properties, Inc. ....PKY
Pennsylvania REIT ....PEI
Phillips International Realty Corp. ....PHR
Plum Creek Timber Company ....PCL
Post Properties, Inc..PPS
Prentiss Properties Trust..PP
Prime Group Realty Trust ....PGE
Prime Retail, Inc. ....PRT
ProLogis ....PLD
Public Storage, Inc...PSA
RAIT Investment Trust ....RAS
Ramco-Gershenson Properties Trust ....RPT
Realty Income Corporation..O
Reckson Associates Realty Corp. ....RA
Redwood Trust, Inc. ....RWT
Regency Centers Corporation..REG
RFS Hotel Investors, Inc..RFS
Rouse Company, The...RSE
Saul Centers, Inc..BFS
Security Capital Group, Inc..SCZ
Senior Housing Properties Trust..SNH
Shurgard Storage Centers, Inc. ....SHU
Simon Property Group, Inc. ....SPG
Sizeler Property Investors, Inc...SIZ
SL Green Realty Corp..SLG
Sovran Self Storage...SSS
Starwood Hotels & Resorts ....HOT
Storage USA, Inc...SUS
Summit Properties, Inc. ....SMT
Sun Communities, Inc. ....SUI
Tanger Factory Outlet Centers, Inc. ....SKT
Taubman Centers, Inc. ....TCO

Thornburg Mortgage Asset Corporation..TMA
Town and Country Trust, The...TCT
Transcontinental Realty Investors, Inc. ....TCI
Trizec Properties, Inc. ....TRZ
U.S. Restaurant Properties ....USV
United Dominion Realty Trust, Inc. ....UDR
Universal Health Realty Income Trust ....UHT
Urstadt Biddle Properties, Inc...UBP
Ventas, Inc...VTR
Vornado Realty Trust ....VNO
Washington Real Estate Investment Trust ....WRE
Weingarten Realty Investors ....WRI
Winston Hotels...WXH

AMERICAN STOCK EXCHANGE
Company Name   **Ticker**
Aegis Realty, Inc...AER
American Mortgage Acceptance Company..............................AMC AMC
AmeriVest Properties, Inc. ....AMV
Anworth Mortgage Asset Corporation...ANH
Arizona Land Income Corporation..AZL
BNP Residential Properties, Inc. ....BNP
Capital Alliance Income Trust..CAA
Commercial Assets, Inc...CAX
FBR Asset Investment Corporation ....FB
Golf Trust of America, Inc...GTA
Hanover Capital Mortgage Holdings, Inc..HCM
Hersha Hospitality Trust...HT
HMG/Courtland Properties, Inc. ....HMG
Impac Commercial Holdings, Inc...ICH
Impac Mortgage Holdings, Inc. ....IMH
Income Opportunity Realty Investors ....IOT
InnSuites Hospitality Trust..IHT
Mission West Properties...MSW
National Health Realty ....NHR
One Liberty Properties, Inc..OLP
Pacific Gateway Properties..PGP
Pittsburgh & West Virginia Rail Road..PW
PMC Commercial Trust ....PCC
Presidential Realty Corporation (Class B) ....PDL B

Price Legacy Corporation...XLG
PS Business Parks, Inc..PSB
Resource Asset Investment Trust ....RAS
Roberts Realty Investors, Inc..RPI
Shelbourne Properties, Inc. I...HXD
Shelbourne Properties, Inc. II..HXE
Shelbourne Properties, Inc. III...HXF
Stonehaven Realty Trust ....RPP
United Mobile Homes, Inc. ....UMH
Wellsford Real Properties, Inc. ....WRP

NASDAQ

Company Name	Ticker
Amresco Capital Trust..	AMCT
Bando McGlockin Capital Corporation	BMCC
Banyan Strategic Realty Trust	BSRTS
Capital Automotive REIT..	CARS
Humphrey Hospitality Trust, Inc......................................	HUMP
Jameson Inns, Inc..	JAMS
Maxus Realty Trust, Inc.	MRTI
Monmouth Real Estate Investment Corp.......................	MNRTA
Pinnacle Holdings, Inc.	BIGT

2

REAL ESTATE LIMITED PARTNERSHIPS

High Income, Tax-Sheltered

L IMITED PARTNERSHIPS are more difficult to invest in than REITs and require a much more serious financial commitment, but they offer some benefits that you can't get with a REIT. And like REITs, they also make it a lot easier to invest in real estate than to buy and manage properties on your own.

"If you are going to invest in real estate on your own, you really need to know and understand the real estate market," explains Robert Fransen, president of Timberland Partners, a Minneapolis-based real estate investment firm. "Most people don't have the time or care to take the time to get to know the real estate market. That's why they are investing in the stock market, because they can get a tip from their broker and just invest. What we provide is the expertise in real estate, and that's why people are investing with us. They want to get involved in real estate, but they don't have the expertise and they don't want to manage all that real estate."

Real estate partnerships give you the opportunity to earn a steady stream of tax-sheltered dividends. And despite their tax-sheltered status, the dividends they pay are higher than nearly any other type of income-oriented investment, including taxable investments such as T-bonds and corporate bonds. In recent years, while most bonds and CDs paid very low yields of about 2 to 5 percent, many real estate partnerships were paying 8 to 13 percent—tax-sheltered.

But there is a catch. Real estate partnerships require a fairly sizable initial investment (often $25,000 to $100,000), and you are generally required to keep your money tied up in the partnership for 5 to 10 years.

Partnerships invest in several types of properties, such as:

- **Apartment complexes**. Among the easiest type of property to buy and manage, apartment complexes offer a steady stream of income from residents. Generally, the partnership hires a manager or management staff to maintain the complex and fill vacancies.

- **Office buildings**. In good economic times, office buildings can be a great source of steady income, but there are some drawbacks, according to Fransen. "You can lose one big tenant, and suddenly you have an empty building that you have to find new tenants for." The other drawback, says Fransen, is that businesses often require very expensive remodeling to meet their requirements. That can dramatically increase up-front costs. If the tenant's business goes badly and it goes belly-up, the limited partnership would have to absorb a large share of those renovation costs—and would have to find another tenant for the building.

- **Warehouses.** This may be the easiest type of commercial property to operate, and can provide a steady flow of income. They typically require little maintenance and little effort to keep occupied (in a normal market).

- **Shopping centers**. Some REITs and limited partnership operations specialize in shopping centers, but they do pose some risks. "This is probably the toughest area of commercial investing," says Fransen. "Shopping centers are very risky. If you put it on the wrong side of the street or you don't have the right mix of retailers, you could be in big trouble."

HOW PARTNERSHIPS WORK

How is a partnership deal put together? They tend to follow a fairly routine pattern. The first step for the partners is to find a good property at a fair price. The partner then makes a down payment of about 20 percent on the total cost, and starts to look for investors. In most cases, the partner already has a list of interested investors before he or she goes out and finds a property.

In many cases, the partnership fixes up their new properties to increase the value and attract a better breed of tenants. The partner also must hire a property manager to run the property and keep the property maintained.

The partner is also responsible for collecting payments from renters and doling out the money to shareholders in the form of dividends.

Finally, it is up to the partner to close out the deal when the partnership has run its course. "In most of our deals," says Fransen, "after 10 years we either have to refinance, sell, or do a tax-deferred exchange for another property. Typically what we do if the value has increased is refinance, take the money out, and buy another building. That way we don't have to pay taxes on the refinance proceeds. We give investors the opportunity to ether take their share out in cash or roll it over into the next deal that we are buying."

WHO SHOULD BUY REAL ESTATE LIMITED PARTNERSHIPS?

Real estate limited partnerships are geared to affluent investors interested in tax-sheltered income who have the ability to set aside a fairly sizable amount of money for a period of several years.

WHO SHOULD *NOT* BUY REAL ESTATE LIMITED PARTNERSHIPS?

If you don't have $10,000 to $100,000 (or more) that you can tie up in an investment for several years, real estate limited partnerships are probably not for you. They are also less than ideal for a tax-sheltered retirement fund because the bulk of the income they provide is already tax-sheltered. Nor would they be appropriate for investors interested in capital appreciation-because they are primarily income-oriented investments.

RETURN

Real estate limited partnerships can be among the most lucrative of all income-oriented investments—particularly among the tax-sheltered options. It is not unusual for limited partnerships to pay 10 percent per year or more in tax-sheltered dividends. And the returns often increase from year to year through the first several years of the partnership.

RISKS

Commercial real estate can deliver excellent returns as long as the real estate market is strong. But in a slow or declining commercial real estate market, you could experience some financial difficulty. If the property owned by your limited partnership runs into high vacancy rates, you could see your income drop dramatically. In fact, in extreme cases, some partnerships have had to go back to shareholders to raise more money to keep properties up and running.

UPSIDE

In addition to their outstanding income, limited partnerships offer several excellent benefits for investors interested in participating in the commercial real estate market:

- **Professional management.** Partnerships are operated by professionals who know what to look for in a property and are able to put a deal together.

- **Increasing stream of income.** Like REITs, limited partnerships often increase their dividends each year, providing investors with a steadily increasing stream of income.

- **Opportunity.** Partnerships give you opportunities to invest in some large properties you probably wouldn't be able to afford on your own

- **Inflation hedge.** Owning real estate can be an inflation hedge. Real estate often rises in value along with inflation, so the value of your investment in real dollars stays about the same regardless of inflation. And the increasing stream of income that limited partnerships provide compensates for the increasing costs of inflation.

- **Management.** "The problem with real estate is that it's management-intensive," says Fransen. The partnership handles all the property management details. They hire property managers to collect the rents, fill vacancies, and handle the maintenance and other responsibilities of commercial property ownership.

- **Tax advantages**. Real estate partnership investors receive some big advantages from the IRS. You can take huge tax credits for the depreciation of the property. "Because of the depreciation, the majority of the cash flow will be sheltered from taxes the first several years," says Fransen. Depreciation rules allow property owners to take large losses (on paper) over the first seven years that the partnership owns the property (and somewhat smaller losses after that). Those losses can be used as tax losses to offset the income you receive from rental income from the property. As a result, all of your returns received during the first several years of the partnership would be tax-free.

DOWNSIDE

While there are some excellent advantages to real estate partnerships, there are also some drawbacks you should know about before investing your money:

- **High cost.** Real estate partnerships are not for small investors. They often require a minimum investment of $25,000 to $50,000, and often higher.

- **Limited opportunities**. You probably wouldn't hear about most real estate partnerships. They are done among a relatively small group of investors generally brought together through a tight network. Unless you have contacts in the business, you may never hear about the good deals.

- **No liquidity**. Once you invest, you better have patience. It could be 5 or 10 years before you can get your money back. Unlike REITs that are traded every day on the stock exchanges, there is no secondary market for limited partnership shares.

- **Subject to market cycles**. As with nearly all types of investments, real estate goes through some fairly dramatic market cycles. Projected returns don't always come through. Rising vacancies can reduce income to investors.

- **Limited diversity**. While some partnerships involve more than one property, others revolve around a single apartment complex, shopping center, or office building. If that property does produce, your returns could suffer.

HOW TO INVEST IN REAL ESTATE PARTNERSHIPS

There is no organized market for real estate limited partnerships. Finding good deals could be difficult unless you're well connected. "You have to know who those people are," says Fransen. "Otherwise, you are not going to have access to the information or the opportunity to invest." To find an opportunity, you may need to ask around, check for real estate investment firms in your area, or talk to your financial advisor. Sometimes brokers have access to limited partnerships or may be able to point you in the right direction, although most would probably try to steer you to a REIT. But a REIT does not offer the same tax advantages that limited partnerships provide. If you want the benefits of a limited partnership, you need to find a company that's in the business.

BIGGEST CONCERNS

Your biggest concern with a real estate limited partnership is the strength of the commercial real estate market. If the market is strong, your investment should do well, but if the bottom drops out of the market, you could see a sharp drop in your income as well as in the value of the properties your partnership owns.

TIMING

Timing is a difficult issue for real estate limited partnerships, in part because they span such a long period of years. Your partnership may own a property for 10 to 15 years, during which real estate goes through two or three economic cycles. These are long-term investments in the truest sense. However, in an ideal world, the best time to become involved in a real estate property is when real estate is in a down market so property prices are depressed. That way, the partnership can buy the property at a discount, and once the market returns, occupancy should go up—along with rent fees—

providing investors with an increasing flow of income. The worst time to buy—although generally impossible to recognize at the time—is at the tail end of a boom market when real estate prices are at record highs. Once the market begins to decline, vacancies increase and your income declines.

MONITORING YOUR LIMITED PARTNERSHIPS

You won't find your partnership's price listed in the newspaper or at any Web site. You must rely on the partnership managers to keep you up-to-date on the status of your investment. Typically, partnerships send out statements to investors periodically. If you need more information on your partnership's performance, you would have to call the partnership manager directly.

ASSET ALLOCATION

As with all types of investments, the amount of your savings that you allocate for real estate limited partnerships would depend on your tax situation, your financial situation, your investment goals, and tolerance for risk. Generally speaking, however, you should put no more than 15 to 25 percent of your assets in a real estate partnership. That should be a fair representation of commercial real estate in a balanced investment portfolio.

SPECIAL CONSIDERATIONS

What should you look for in a partnership deal?

The first consideration is the management. Does the partnership firm have a solid track record? Ask for references if necessary, and call them to see if they have been satisfied with their investments with that partnership group.

You also should review the anticipated return on investment. What will your annual payout rate be and how does that compare with other investments. You want a return that compares favorably with other partnership deals and that has a bigger payout than most bonds and other fixed income assets.

You should also check out the investor pack given to you by the partnership firm. According to Fransen, the information packet would typically include "information about the marketplace, comparable rent survey, how we are going to finance it, how we expect it to operate, and what we anticipate our returns to be. We may also include some sort of exit strategy in that."

Finally, you might want to take a look at the property itself. "We do have some investors who go out and look over the properties themselves, but we also have some people who never look at the properties. They just trust our judgment." If the management's track record has been good, you may not need to do a property visit, but for your own curiosity and peace of mind, you might want to go check out the property yourself. After all, you'll soon be a part owner, and this is no small investment.

3

U.S. SAVINGS BONDS (SERIES EE)
Safety and Adjustable Income

O NE OF THE SIMPLEST investments available to small investors is the U.S. Savings Bond, Series EE. They are easy to buy, and they are available in much smaller denominations than other types of bonds. You can buy a savings bond for as little as $25.

Although savings bonds do not pay a high return, the interest they earn is exempt from state and local taxes. You can also get some additional tax savings if you use the bonds for education. Depending on your income, interest earned from the bond is either fully or partially exempt from federal taxes if you use it for college tuition for yourself or your children.

There are some important differences between U.S. Savings Bonds and other types of bonds. The most common type of savings bond is the Series EE. Those bonds are issued at half their face value. For instance, when you buy a $100 bond, you pay $50 for it. They pay no interest; instead you receive earnings from the bond when you redeem it. So when you redeem a $100 bond—which you paid $50 to buy—you receive the full $100.

In addition to Series EE, the government also offers the Patriot Bond, which was issued after 9/11 and is nearly identical to the Series EE bonds.

One other option is the Series HH bonds, although you can't buy Series HH bonds with cash—you can only get them in exchange for Series EE bonds or upon reinvestment of the proceeds of matured Series H bonds.

Unlike Series EE bonds, Series HH bonds are current-income securities, which means they don't increase in value. Instead, they pay a regular interest payment every six months. When an HH bond is issued, you pay the face amount ($500, $1000, $5000, or $10,000) for the bond. The interest payments on HH bonds are made by direct deposit to your checking or savings account at a financial institution.

The government also recently began offering an "I bond," which is geared to investors seeking to protect the purchasing power of their investment and earn a guaranteed real rate of return. Unlike traditional savings bonds, I bonds are sold at face value and grow in value with a varying interest rate tied to the rate of inflation. (More on I bonds in the next chapter.)

Savings bonds are not limited to the length of their term. In fact, you can redeem them any time—from within 12 months of buying them to as long as 30 years later. After a savings bond reaches its original maturity, it automatically enters one or more extension periods, usually of 10-years' duration. Savings bonds stop earning interest when they reach final maturity. For Series EE bonds, final maturity is 30 years, and for Series HH bonds, it is 20 years.

The interest rate on Series EE bonds is not fixed. Instead, they earn interest based on 90 percent of the average yields of five-year Treasury securities for the preceding six months. U.S. Savings Bonds increase in value every month, and interest is compounded semiannually. Series HH bonds, on the other hand, have a set rate of interest that does not change until the investor has held the bond for 10 years.

WHO SHOULD BUY U.S. SAVINGS BONDS?

Savings bonds are geared to small, conservative investors interested in safety, capital appreciation, and tax savings.

WHO SHOULD *NOT* BUY U.S. SAVINGS BONDS?

Series EE bonds would not be attractive to investors looking for income or aggressive investors looking for capital appreciation.

RETURN

The return from U.S. Savings Bonds is not especially enticing, although the exemption from state and local taxes does help enhance the return. For the long-term, U.S. Savings Bonds fall far behind stocks—about 4.8 percent per year for savings bonds versus 10.7 percent for stocks.

Series EE bonds have a variable rate that changes every six months. The rate is based on 90 percent of the average of prevailing market yields on five-year Treasury securities. So if five-year Treasury securities are paying 5 percent, a Series EE bond would pay 4.5 percent. A new rate is announced each May and November that reflects average market yields during the preceding six-month period. Because the interest rate for Series EE bonds is a market-based, variable rate, there is no way to predict when a bond will reach face value. However, Series EE bonds are guaranteed to reach maturity within 17 years.

Interest does not begin to accrue until the fourth month after the bond is issued. Then it accrues on the first day of each month. Interest is paid when the bonds are redeemed. If a Series EE bond is redeemed less than five years after the date of issue, the overall earning period from the date of issue will be reduced by three months.

Series HH bonds, on the other hand, pay interest at a fixed rate set on the day you buy the bond. Interest rates are reset on the 10th anniversary of the HH bonds' issue date. The interest rate is generally very low. Series HH bond buyers in 2003 received an annual rate of 1.5 percent locked in for 10 years. At the same time, Series EE bonds were paying 3.25 percent.

Unlike Series EE bonds, Series HH bonds are current-income securities, which means the HH bond itself doesn't increase in value. When an HH bond is issued, the investor pays the face amount ($500, $1000, $5000, or $10,000) for the bond and interest is paid every six months. The interest payments on HH bonds are made by direct deposit to the investor's checking or savings account. (See Figures 3-1 and 3-2.)

RISKS

There are almost no risks associated with owning U.S. Savings Bonds. They are almost as safe as cash itself because they are backed by the full faith and credit of the federal government.

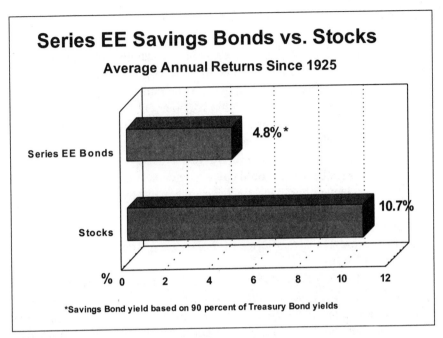

FIGURE 3-1

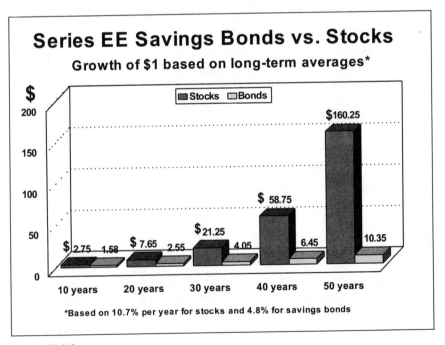

FIGURE 3-2

UPSIDE

There are many benefits to owning U.S. savings bonds. The biggest benefit is safety. Because they are backed by the U.S. government, they are considered to be among the safest investments in the world. Here are some other positives:

- **Tax benefits**. Earnings from savings bonds is exempt from state and local taxes, and, if used for college tuition, it is also exempt from federal taxes.

- **No interest payments**. You don't receive interest payments, so you don't need to claim your gains and pay taxes each year. You defer paying federal income taxes on the earnings until you cash it in.

- **Easy to buy**. Savings bonds are easy to buy. You can get them at nearly any bank, and you pay no commission (although the bonds do not begin earning interest until three months after they are issued).

- **Liquidity**. You can cash in the bonds any time after the first 12 months, although if you cash them in during the first five years, there is a penalty equivalent of three months interests.

- **Variable rate**. Although you may hold a bond 20 to 30 years, you are not locked in to the same rate. You can buy savings bonds during periods of low rates, and their interest will rise in the years ahead as market interest rates rise, whereas with most bonds, the interest rate never changes.

DOWNSIDE

The downside to savings bonds is the return. It's low for Series EE Savings Bonds and horrible for Series HH bonds. What could possibly motivate anyone to buy a Series HH bond with a rate of 1.5 percent locked in for 10 years? Series EE bonds offer a little better rate (3.25 percent in 2003), but it's still not much higher than the rate of inflation.

If you're looking for income, Series EE bonds are not for you. They pay no income, but rather appreciate in value, with the payoff coming when you cash in the bonds.

HOW TO BUY U.S. SAVINGS BONDS

U.S. Savings Bonds may be purchased directly from the Treasury or from commercial banks. They are also often available through employee savings plans. And in recent years, they have been offered over the Internet through some online brokers, and through the federal government. The best source on the Internet is a site sponsored by the U.S. Treasury: *www.savings-bonds.gov.*

When you buy a savings bond, you receive a registered savings bond certificate. There is no secondary market for savings bonds. They can not be resold or even given away.

Savings bonds are geared to small investors and come in denominations of $50, $75, $100, $200, $500, $1000, $5000, and $10,000. Investors may not purchase more than $30,000 worth of Series EE U.S. Savings Bonds per year, although you can also buy up to $30,000 in I Bonds, as well, totaling a maximum of $60,000 annually. Savings bonds earn interest for 30 years from the issue date.

There is a penalty for cashing in an EE Bond before it is five years old. The penalty is a deduction of three months' interest in the final payout. You are also prohibited from cashing in a Series EE bond within 12 months of purchase.

Series HH bonds are more difficult to buy—and hardly worth the effort. You can't buy HH bonds with cash. You can get them only in exchange for Series EE or Series E bonds or upon reinvestment of the proceeds of matured Series H bonds. When an HH bond is issued, you pay the face amount ($500, $1000, $5000, or $10,000) for the bond and interest is paid every six months, providing you with "current income." HH Bonds are issued in denominations of $500, $1000, $5000, and $10,000.

BIGGEST CONCERNS

U.S. Savings Bonds are very predictable investments. What you see is what you get. Because there is no secondary market for savings bonds, there's no concern about trading losses, and because they are issued and backed by the federal government, there's no concern about loss of capital investment.

TIMING

The best time to buy savings bonds is when interest rates are low and may be heading higher. Most other bonds carry a fixed rate, so you're stuck with the initial rate throughout the life of the bond—even if that's for 30 years. With Series EE U.S. Savings Bonds, the interest rate is adjusted every six months to reflect any changes in market interest rates. So if market rates are going up, the rate you'll receive from your Series EE bond will also go up.

By contrast, the worst time to buy savings bonds is when interest rates are high and may be heading back down. It would be better at that point to buy a conventional bond to lock in the high rate. With a Series EE bond, as the prevailing market interest rate drops, so does the yield you would earn on your savings bond.

MONITORING YOUR SAVINGS BONDS

Because you can't sell your savings bonds on a secondary market, savings bond prices never change. However, the yield changes every six months, so you might want to find out what interest rate your bond is paying for that period. You can find current rates and volumes of other information about savings bonds and other government bonds at the federal government's own Web site—*www.treasurydirect.gov*, or you can go directly to the section on savings bonds at *www.savingsbonds.gov*.

ASSET ALLOCATION

How much of your assets should be invested in savings bonds? As with all types of investments, asset allocation depends on your own goals and threshold for risk.

Conservative investors who are more concerned with preservation of capital than they are with growth might want 5 to 20 percent of their assets in savings bonds—if interest rates are low. If interest rates are high, you should cut back your allocation in savings bonds and add to conventional long-term bonds so you can lock in the high rate.

Aggressive investors looking for long-term growth would probably want to avoid savings bonds altogether. Perhaps, when interest rates are very low and starting to rise, you might want to put a small percentage of your assets in savings bonds rather than other fixed income investments. But other types of investments offer more potential for growth over the long term.

SPECIAL CONSIDERATIONS

Savings bonds offer extra benefits for education. If applied to college expenses, savings bond earnings are exempt from federal taxes. If you're considering buying bonds for this purpose, it is not necessary to declare that they will be used for education when you buy the bonds. When using bonds for a child's education, register the bonds in your name—not the child's (nor can a child be listed as co-owner of the bond). If you are married, you must file a joint return to qualify for the education exclusion. Not everyone qualifies for this exemption. If your gross adjusted income is more than $83,650 for married taxpayers or $55,750 for single taxpayers, you would qualify for only a partial, prorated deduction. If you make over $113,650 for married couples or $70,750 for singles, you would not be able to claim any deduction for education.

C H A P T E R

I BONDS (SERIES I U.S. SAVINGS BONDS)

Safety and Inflation-Adjusted Income

I N **1998,** the federal government introduced a new type of U.S. Savings Bond tied to the rate of inflation. The new bonds are known as "I Bonds," and, like Series EE bonds, they are easy to buy, and they are available in much smaller denominations than other types of bonds. You can buy an I Bond savings bond for as little as $50.

I Bonds do not pay interest, but rather appreciate in value until the bondholder cashes them in.

There are many similarities between Series EE bonds and I Bonds. For instance, the interest earned from I Bonds is exempt from state and local taxes. You can also get some additional tax savings if you use the bonds for education. Depending on your income, interest earned from the bond is either fully or partially exempt from federal taxes if you use it for college tuition for yourself or your children.

But unlike Series EE bonds, I Bonds are sold at face value (a $100 bond costs $100), whereas Series EE bonds are issued at 50 percent of face value. But like Series EE bonds, I Bonds pay no current interest; instead you receive earnings from the bond when you redeem it.

I Bonds are not limited to the length of their term. In fact, you can redeem them any time—from within 12 months of buying them to as long as 30 years later. After a savings bond reaches its original maturity, it automatically enters one or more extension periods, usually of 10 years' duration. I Bonds stop earning interest when they reach final maturity, which is at 30 years,

Like Series EE bonds, the interest rate paid on I Bonds is not fixed. Instead, it is based on both a fixed base rate of return plus an adjustable semiannual inflation rate tied to the Consumer Price Index (CPI). The CPI is one way the government measures inflation. As consumer prices increase, so does the CPI. And as the CPI increases, so does the rate offered by I Bonds. Interest rates paid by I Bonds are adjusted every six months. Although I Bonds tend to pay a lower rate than market rates offered by other types of bonds, the adjustable rate feature assures you that your I Bond return will always outpace the rate of inflation.

WHO SHOULD BUY I BONDS?

I Bonds are geared to conservative investors interested in safety, capital appreciation, tax savings, and a hedge against inflation. With their small denominations, they are ideal for small individual investors.

WHO SHOULD *NOT* BUY I BONDS?

I Bonds would not be attractive to investors looking for income or aggressive investors looking for capital appreciation.

RETURN

The rate of return offered by I Bonds is not particularly attractive, although the tax benefits and inflation protection help compensate for the lower rate. Like Series EE Savings Bonds, I Bonds tend to pay a lower rate than corporate and U.S. Treasury bonds.

The return from I Bonds can be higher or lower than Series EE bonds, depending on a number of factors, including the rate of inflation and market interest rates. For instance, in the first half of 2003, I Bonds paid 4.08 percent, while Series EE Bonds paid 3.25 percent. But in the previous six-month period, Series EE bonds paid a higher rate—3.96 percent compared with 2.57 percent for I Bonds.

The rate for I Bonds is adjusted for inflation every six months. The rate is set through a rather complex calculation. Series I bonds accrue earnings based on a combination of the fixed interest rate and the semiannual inflation rate. The government announces the composite rate each May and November.

The government uses the monthly nonseasonally adjusted *U.S. City Average All Items Consumer Price Index for All Urban Consumers* (CPI-U) published by the Bureau of Labor Statistics of the U.S. Department of Labor to determine the inflation rate. For example, the semiannual inflation rate to be effective with a Treasury announcement in May of each year reflects the rate of change in the CPI-U for the six-month period ending with the immediately preceding February. The CPI-U represents prices of all goods and services purchased for consumption by urban households. User fees (such as water and sewer service) and sales and excise taxes paid by the consumer are also included. Income taxes and investment items (stocks, bonds, and life insurance) are not included. The CPI-U includes expenditures by urban wage earners and clerical workers, professional, managerial, and technical workers, the self-employed, short-term workers, the unemployed, retirees, and others not in the labor force.

The return offered by I Bonds would be very low during periods of low inflation or deflation because negative as well as positive changes in the CPI-U are used to calculate composite rates. In fact, the return could fall to 0 percent during a deflationary period. If deflation were such that it more than fully offset the fixed rate of return and produced a negative composite rate, the government would not reduce the composite rate below zero. In this event, the redemption value of a Series I bond would remain constant through the period and become the base for calculating earnings that might accrue during the subsequent period.

Because I Bonds were first issued in 1998, it is impossible to provide a long-term comparison between their rate of return and the return from stocks. But other U.S. Savings Bonds have trailed the stock market averages dramatically over the long-term. For the long-term, U.S. Savings Bonds have provided about a 4.8 percent per year return compared with a 10.7 percent average annual return for stocks.

Interest on I Bonds does not begin to accrue until the fourth month after the bond is issued. Then it accrues on the first day of each month. The redemption value of a bond does not change between accrual dates. A Series I bond may be redeemed beginning 12 months after it's issued. Interest is paid when the bonds are redeemed. If an I Bond is redeemed less than five years after the date of issue, the overall earning period from the date of issue will be reduced by three months.

RISKS

There are almost no risks associated with owning I Bonds. Like all U.S. Savings Bonds, they are almost as safe as cash itself because they are backed by the full faith and credit of the federal government.

UPSIDE

There are many benefits to owning I Bonds. The biggest benefits are inflation protection and safety. Because they are backed by the U.S. government, they are considered to be among the safest investments in the world. Here are some important benefits:

- **Inflation adjustment**. Although you may hold a bond for 20 to 30 years, you are not locked into the same rate. If inflation picks up, the return from your I Bond will also increase to compensate for the jump in inflation. By contrast, for most bonds, the interest rate never changes.

- **Tax savings.** Earnings from I Bonds is exempt from state and local taxes, and, if used for college tuition, it is also exempt from federal taxes.

- **No interest payments**. You don't receive interest payments, so you don't need to claim your gains and pay taxes each year. You defer paying federal income taxes on the earnings until you cash in the bond.

- **Easy to buy.** I Bonds are easy to buy. You can get them at nearly any bank or online, and you pay no commission (although the bonds do not begin earning interest until three months after they are issued).

- **Liquidity.** You can cash in I Bonds any time after the first 12 months, although if you cash them in during the first five years, there is a penalty equivalent to three months' interest.

DOWNSIDE

The downside to I Bonds is that they pay a fairly low interest rate compared with corporate and U.S. Treasury bonds. The interest rate paid by I Bonds is similar to Series EE Savings Bonds, but may be higher or lower depending on the inflation rate and market interest rates.

If you're looking for income, I Bonds are not for you. They pay no income, but rather appreciate in value, with the payoff coming when you cash in the bonds.

HOW TO BUY I BONDS

I Bonds may be purchased directly from the Treasury or from commercial banks. They are also often available through employee savings plans. And in recent years, they have been offered over the Internet through some online brokers, and through the federal government. The best source on the Internet is a site sponsored by the U.S. Treasury: *www.savingsbonds.gov.*

When you buy an I Bond, you receive a registered savings bond certificate. There is no secondary market for savings bonds. They cannot be resold or even given away.

I Bonds are geared to small investors and come in denominations of $50, $75, $100, $200, $500, $1000, $5000, and $10,000. Investors may not purchase more than $30,000 worth of I Bonds per year, although you can also buy $30,000 worth of Series EE U.S. Savings Bonds per year, totaling a maximum of $60,000 annually. I Bonds can earn interest for a maximum of 30 years from the issue date.

There is a penalty for cashing in your I Bond before it is five years old. The penalty is a deduction of three months' interest in the final payout. You are also prohibited from cashing in I Bonds within 12 months of purchase.

BIGGEST CONCERNS

I Bonds are very simple, predictable investments. Because there is no secondary market for I Bonds, there's no concern about trading losses, and because they are issued and backed by the federal government, there's no concern about loss of capital investment. The biggest concern would be deflation. In a period of deflation, the return from I Bonds could drop to 0 percent. However, deflation has not been a factor in the United States in more than a century, so the risk of deflation cutting your return to zero would be very low. However, a low inflation rate could keep your returns at a very low level.

TIMING

The best time to buy I Bonds would be during a period of rising inflation. Because the interest rate rises as inflation rises, I Bonds would work better during high inflation than fixed-rate securities, which pay the same interest rate through maturity—which can be for up to 30 years.

By contrast, the worst time to buy I Bonds is when inflation is low and falling. During times of declining inflation, the return on I Bonds declines as well. At those times, you would be better served to buy a fixed-rate bond, and lock into a guaranteed long-term rate.

MONITORING YOUR I BONDS

Because you can't sell your I Bonds on a secondary market, their prices never change. However, the yield changes every six months, so you might want to find out what interest rate your bond is paying for that period. You can find current rates and volumes of other information about savings bonds and other government bonds at the federal government's own Web site—*www.treasurydirect.gov*, or you can go directly to the section on savings bonds at *www.savingsbonds.gov*.

ASSET ALLOCATION

As with all types of investments, the amount of your savings that you allocate for I Bonds would depend on your tax situation, your financial situation, your investment goals, and threshold for risk.

Conservative investors who are more concerned with preservation of spending power than they are with growth might want to invest 5 to 25 percent of their assets in I Bonds under normal economic conditions. You might want to lighten the weighting of I Bonds in the portfolio during periods of low inflation, and increase the weighting during periods of rising inflation.

Investors interested in income would probably not include I Bonds (or Series EE bonds) in their portfolio because they do not provide any interest payments.

Aggressive investors looking for long-term growth would probably want to avoid I Bonds most of the time. However, during periods of rising inflation, I Bonds might make a good investment as part of a diversified portfolio. But there would be no reason to invest more than 5 to 10 percent of assets in I Bonds if you're an aggressive investor.

SPECIAL CONSIDERATIONS

I Bonds are not the investment to hold if the economy ever slips into a deflationary period. The return could be as low as zero.

I Bonds offer the same benefits for education that Series EE bonds provide. If applied to college expenses, I Bond earnings are exempt from federal taxes. If you're considering buying bonds for this purpose, it is not necessary to declare that they will be used for education when you buy the bonds. When using bonds for a child's education, register the bonds in your name—not the child's (nor can a child be listed as co-owner of the bond). If you are married, you must file a joint return to qualify for the education exclusion. Not everyone qualifies for this exemption. If your gross adjusted income is more than $83,650 for married taxpayers or $55,750 for single taxpayers, you would qualify for only a partial, prorated deduction. If you make over $113,650 for married couples or $70,750 for singles, you would not be able to claim any deduction for education.

U.S. TREASURY BONDS AND NOTES

Safety and Income

FOR A STEADY STREAM of income, bonds are your most obvious option. But there are many different types of bonds, each with a slightly different level of risk and return on investment. Generally speaking, the safer the bond, the lower the yield.

Two of the safest and most popular bonds on the market are U.S. Treasury Bonds (T-bonds) and Treasury Notes (T-notes). In fact, all U.S. Treasury debt securities, including bonds, bills, and notes, are considered to be virtually immune from default because they are backed by the safest entity on earth—the U.S. government. Even if the government doesn't have the funds to pay off its securities, it can simply print more money.

The government stopped issuing 30-year bonds in 2001, but you can still buy them on the secondary bond market.

The Treasury continues to issue notes, which are identical to bonds in nearly every respect except length of maturity (and yield). While bonds were issued only with 30-year maturities, notes come in shorter terms, including 2 years, 3 years, 5 years, 7 years, and 10 years.

Although the federal government is the largest issuer of bonds, it is certainly not the only entity that uses bonds to raise money. They are also popular with state and municipal entities as well as most major corporations. Bonds typically pay interest every six months throughout the term of the bond. Bonds "mature" at the end of a prespecified term, at which time the bondholder receives an amount equal to his or her original investment (the "principal"). For instance, T-bonds were issued with a 30-year maturity—the longest of all government bonds—which meant that they paid a preset amount of interest each year for 30 years before the principal was returned to the bondholders.

The excessive length of maturity of the 30-year bonds kept many buyers away, which is why the government discontinued selling those bonds in 2001. With their shorter maturities, T-Notes had become much more popular than T-Bonds.

In addition to the safe, steady income Treasury securities provide, they also offer one other alluring benefit—the interest they pay is exempt from state and local taxes. Because of the separation of federal and state powers mandated by the U.S. Constitution, states cannot tax federal securities—and the federal government cannot tax state and local securities. That tax exemption makes the after-tax return from Treasury securities much more attractive. However, interest from bonds and notes is still subject to federal income taxes.

T-bonds and notes may not appeal to investors looking for the highest possible return, but if you're looking for safety, they're hard to beat.

WHO SHOULD BUY TREASURY BONDS?

T-bonds and notes are ideal for conservative investors interested in safety, income, and a break on their state and local taxes. But more aggressive investors might also be interested in them because they can help provide diversification for their portfolio.

WHO SHOULD *NOT* BUY TREASURY BONDS?

Treasury bonds would not be attractive to investors looking for a high level of income or capital appreciation.

RETURN

Since 1925, long-term government bonds have provided an average annual return of about 5.3 percent. That is a better rate than money market funds, Treasury bills, and most short-term fixed income investments, such as certificates of deposit. However, T-bonds trail corporate bonds, which have averaged about 5.8 percent since 1925, and high-yield (junk) bonds that tend to offer yields of 2 to 4 points higher than the AAA-rated corporate bonds. The 5.3 percent average annual return earned by T-bonds is about half the return from blue chip stocks, which have averaged 10.7 percent per year.

However, because of their tax-favored status (T-bonds and notes are exempt from state and local taxes), the relative return they offer would be slightly higher than 5.3 percent. The bonds of choice for real tax savings are municipal bonds, which are exempt from federal taxes—and, in some cases, state taxes, as well. But the average annual return from municipal bonds has been a paltry 4.2 percent.

Returns for T-bonds and notes can vary greatly from year to year. The yields hit double-digits in the early 1980s—as high as 14 percent—but dropped to less than 5 percent in 2003. T-bonds have provided a significantly higher yield than T-notes. In 2003, while T-bonds were paying about 4.9 percent, 10-year notes were paying only about 3.9 percent. The shorter the maturity, the lower the yield. Seven-year notes were paying 3.44 percent, 5-year notes were at 2.85 percent, 3-year notes were at 1.87 percent, and 2-year notes were at just 1.56 percent.

Interest rates are determined based on bids from bond buyers at regular auctions held by the U.S. Treasury. Bond rates have tracked fairly closely with the "prime rate," which is a benchmark loan rate banks charge to their best commercial customers.

Figures 5-1 and 5-2 illustrate the comparison between long-term Treasury bonds and blue chip stocks.

RISKS

There are almost no risks associated with owning T-bonds and notes. Like all government-issued debt instruments, they are almost as safe as cash itself because they are backed by the full faith and credit of the federal government.

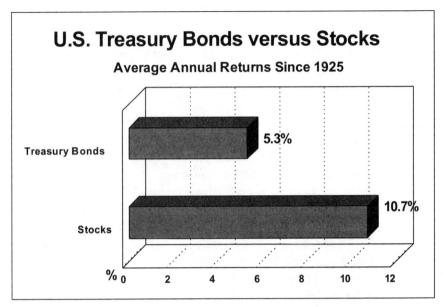

FIGURE 5-1

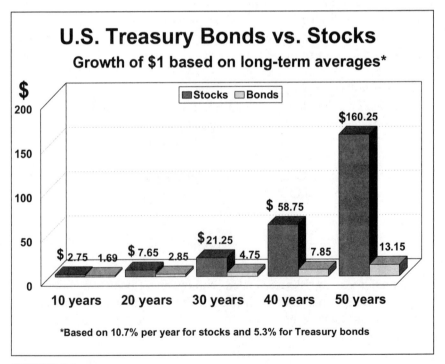

FIGURE 5-2

UPSIDE

There are several important benefits of owning T-bonds and notes. Safety and a steady stream of income are the most obvious, but there are some other benefits, as well, such as:

- **Tax savings.** Earnings are exempt from state and local taxes.

- **Non-callable.** T-Bonds are not callable, which means the Treasury cannot redeem them before maturity—unlike bonds issued by many corporations and municipalities.

- **Liquidity.** A huge secondary market for Treasury securities makes it easy to buy and sell them whenever you wish. If you don't want to hold them through maturity, it's easy to find a buyer on the secondary market.

- **Easy to buy.** T-Notes are easy to buy and can be purchased through your bank, your broker, or the U.S. Treasury.

DOWNSIDE

The downside to T-bonds and notes is that they pay a fairly low interest rate compared with corporate bonds, although they do typically pay a higher rate than shorter-term government securities, such as Treasury Bills.

Unless you plan to hold your T-bond for the full 30 years (or your notes for the full length of maturity), there is also a risk of loss of principal. Bonds tend to decline in value during times of rising interest rates. For instance, if you bought a T-bond with a 5-percent rate of return, and interest rates have climbed steadily to 10 percent, no one would be interested in buying your 5-percent bond at the full rate. You would have to sell the bond at a discount, costing you a portion of your principal. On the other hand, if interest rates are dropping—you bought the bond with a 10-percent rate, and interest rates dropped to 5 percent—you could sell your bond at a premium, earning a nice profit on the sale.

HOW TO BUY T-BONDS AND NOTES

Treasury Notes may be purchased for $1000 or higher in multiples of $1000. Treasury Bonds were issued in denominations of $1000, $5000,

$10,000, $100,000, and $1 million. Investors pay the face amount for Treasuries ($1000 for a $1000 bond) and receive interest checks every six months. If you wish, you can have your interest payment mailed to you in the form of a check, or deposited automatically in your checking or savings account.

Two-year notes are issued at the end of each month, and 3-year, 5-year, and 10-year notes are issued on February 15, May 15, August 15, and November 15 of each year.

You can purchase Treasury securities through a bank, a broker, or—for those who prefer to pay no commission—directly from the U.S. Treasury. To buy from the Treasury, you would go directly through a Federal Reserve branch or the Bureau of Public Debt (1300 C St., S.W., Washington, DC 20239).

In order to buy directly from the Fed, you need to put in a "noncompetitive bid" at the Treasury's quarterly auction (they occur in February, May, August, and November), which means you are willing to pay the average rate for the securities you want. Otherwise you can buy a Treasury security through a regular bank or brokerage firm for a fee of about $50. They can also be easily bought and sold on the secondary bond market.

Perhaps the most convenient way to buy Treasury securities is through the U.S. Treasury's Web site, *www.treasurydirect.gov*. You can go to the site, click on the section for "Treasury Bills, Notes and Bonds," and follow the instructions. You'll be able to buy treasury securities online, directly from the U.S. Treasury without paying a commission.

BIGGEST CONCERNS

For conservative investors who plan to hold for the full term of the bond, Treasuries offer little reason for concern. However, if you buy a T-bond or note while interest rates are low, you could be stuck with a low yield for a very long time. In fact, if you hold your bond through a period of rising inflation, your yield could actually fall below the rate of inflation. That means, in real dollar terms, your wealth would actually be declining instead of increasing with each interest payment.

To avoid the creep of inflation, you could sell your bonds as interest rates rise, but that would mean taking a hit on the price of the bond. You would be forced to sell the bond for less than what you paid for it. So while Treasuries are safe and secure in principal, they can have some risks.

TIMING

The best time to buy Treasuries, as with nearly all traditional types of bonds, would be during periods of high interest rates. It can be difficult to predict the movement of interest rates, but as interest rates drop, the value of existing bonds increases. Buying bonds near the peak of interest rates would put you in a very strong position. As interest rates drop, you could hold the bond and continue to enjoy high returns, or you could sell the bond at a premium, earning a tidy profit on your investment.

By contrast, the worst time to buy Treasuries would be during a period when interest rates are low and are beginning to rise. That would put you in the unenviable position of either collecting low rates throughout the term of the bond, or selling it out at a loss. You could opt for bonds with shorter terms, but the shorter the term, the worse the return. For instance, in 2003, two-year Treasury Notes were paying just 1.56 percent compared to 3.94 percent for 10-year notes and 4.94 percent for 30-year bonds. When rates are low, your options are all less than ideal.

MONITORING YOUR TREASURIES

T-bond and T-note rates and prices are listed in the *Wall Street Journal*, *Investors' Business Daily*, and other financial publications. You can find current rates and volumes of other information about savings bonds and other government bonds at the federal government's own Web site— *www.treasurydirect.gov*. Yield data and other information is also listed at a number of other Web sites, including *www.investinginbonds.com*, *www.bondsonline.com*, and *www.forecasts.org*.

ASSET ALLOCATION

The amount of money you allocate toward U.S. Treasury Bonds and Notes would depend on your tax situation, your financial situation, your investment goals, and your threshold for risk.

Conservative investors who are more concerned with preservation of spending power than they are with growth might want to invest 20 to 50 percent of their assets in T-bonds and notes under normal economic conditions. You might want to lighten the weighting of Treasuries in the portfolio during periods of low interest rates, and increase the weighting during periods of high interest.

Aggressive investors looking for long-term growth would probably want to limit their investment in T-Bonds and notes, particularly in times of low interest. However, an allocation of 5 to 20 percent of assets in government bonds and notes even for aggressive investors would help provide balance and diversification, and could buoy the portfolio when stocks are down.

SPECIAL CONSIDERATIONS

If you want to own T-bonds, but you don't want to be tied to them for 25 to 30 years, you can buy bonds on the bond market that are closer to maturity. For instance, let's say interest rates are fairly low, and you are concerned that rates may go up over the next few years. You would prefer not to commit to a bond for a 20- to 30-year period. Through the bond market, you can buy a bond from someone else who may have purchased that bond 10 to 20 years ago and now wants to sell it. If you buy a bond in the secondary market that matures earlier than 30 years, that would limit your risk. If interest rates were to increase, you would be stuck with the lower rate for a shorter period of time. Then, once the bond matured, you could cash it out and buy a new bond at a higher yield. You could also go with the shorter-term notes or bills, but you have to settle for a significantly lower yield.

6

TIPS (TREASURY INFLATION-PROTECTED SECURITIES)

Safety and Inflation-Adjusted Income

TO ATTRACT INVESTORS during low-interest environments, the federal government introduced a new type of Treasury security recently that increases in value and payout along with the rate of inflation. The new bonds, technically known as Treasury Inflation-Indexed Securities, are referred to as *TIPS* (an acronym for Treasury Inflation-Protected Securities). TIPS are designed to help you maintain the true worth of your investment regardless of the rate of inflation.

Like other Treasury securities, TIPS pay interest twice a year and are exempt from state and local taxes. They are issued in 10-year terms.

During times of inflation, TIPS not only pay a higher return, they also increase in value. The principal increases, so when they reach maturity, you would receive more money than you actually paid in initially.

Here is how TIPS work:

Using the Consumer Price Index as a guide, the value of the principal is adjusted to reflect the effects of inflation. A fixed interest rate is paid semiannually on the adjusted amount. At maturity, if inflation has increased the value of the principal, the investor receives the higher value. If deflation has decreased the value, the investor nevertheless receives the original face amount of the security.

For instance, let's say you invested $1000 in a 10-year inflation-indexed note paying 3 percent interest. At midyear, the Consumer Price Index indicates that inflation has been 1 percent during the first six months. Your principal is adjusted upward to $1010, and your interest payment (one-half of 3 percent) is based on that figure. Your payment is $15.15. At the end of the year, the index indicates that inflation was 3 percent, which brings the value of your principal to $1030. Your second interest payment is $15.45 ($1030 times 3 percent divided by 2).

Here are some other important tips on TIPS:

- The interest rate, which is set at auction, remains fixed throughout the term of the security.

- The principal amount of the security is adjusted for inflation, but the inflation-adjusted principal will not be paid until maturity.

- Semiannual interest payments are based on the inflation-adjusted principal at the time the interest is paid.

- The index for measuring the inflation rate is the nonseasonally adjusted U.S. City Average All Items Consumer Price Index for All Urban Consumers (CPI-U), published monthly by the Bureau of Labor Statistics (BLS).

- The auction process uses a single-price auction method that is the same as that currently used for all of Treasury's marketable securities auctions.

- At maturity, the securities will be redeemed at the greater of their inflation-adjusted principal or par amount at original issue.

Although TIPS tend to pay a lower interest rate initially than T-bonds or notes, that could change over the term of the bond. Either way, the adjustable rate feature assures you that your TIPS will always outpace inflation.

WHO SHOULD BUY TIPS?

TIPS are geared to conservative investors interested in safety, income, tax savings, and a hedge against inflation. Aggressive investors might also be interesed in TIPS because they provide diversification for the portfolio.

WHO SHOULD *NOT* BUY TIPS?

TIPS would not be attractive to investors looking for capital appreciation or aggressive investors looking for a higher annual return.

RETURN

The initial rate of return offered by TIPS is somewhat lower than T-bonds and notes, but over the term of the TIPS bond, its return could exceed that of other Treasury securities. And, at the end of the term, the principal would be higher than the principal from other traditional Treasury securities, such as bonds and notes, that carry a fixed interest rate and a fixed principal. Because the TIPS principal grows with inflation, your principal at the end of the 10-year term could be significantly higher than it was at the beginning.

All things considered, TIPS would appear to be a much better value than T-Notes—particularly during times of high inflation.

Here is a comparison of interest rates for T-Bonds, T-Notes, and TIPS:

- A TIPS 10-year note paid about 3 percent in 2003 compared with 3.9 percent offered by 10-year T-Notes.

- A 10-year TIPS with 7 years to maturity was paying 4.25 percent compared with a 7-year T-Note that paid 3.44 percent.

- A 10-year TIPS with 5 years remaining to maturity paid 3.63 percent compared with a 5-year T-Note that paid 2.85 percent.

- The 30-year TIPS were paying about 3.38 percent compared with the 30-year T-bond, which was paying about 4.9 percent. Although that may seem like a dramatic difference for the 30-year instruments, a tremendous amount of inflation can occur over a 30-year period. By the end of the 30-year term, the inflation-adjusted TIPS principal could grow by 50 to 80 percent—along with the semiannual interest payment.

To adjust the TIPS principal, the government uses the Consumer Price Index as a guide. The value of the principal is adjusted to reflect the effects of inflation. The interest rate itself is fixed for the life of the bond, but that interest rate accounts for a higher actual payment each time the principal increases.

Specifically, each interest payment (two per year) is calculated by multiplying the inflation-indexed principal by one-half the fixed interest rate determined at auction when the bond was issued.

For example, let's say you're holding a $1000 TIPS with a 4-percent interest rate, and inflation is up 2 percent. You would multiply the $1000 principal by 2 percent, which equals $20, and add that $20 to the principal, giving you a principal of $1020. Then multiply that times your 4-percent fixed annual interest rate, which equals $40.80. Since you receive half of your interest every six months, you would divide that annualized sum in half, giving you a semiannual payment of $20.40 cents.

At maturity, if inflation has increased the value of the principal, the investor receives the higher value. If deflation has decreased the value, the investor nevertheless receives the original face amount of the security.

RISKS

TIPS are one of the safest investments ever conceived. Not only are they essentially free from default because they are backed by the full faith and credit of the federal government, they are also insulated against the effects of inflation. You are virtually assured that the value of your investment will not decline. Even during times of deflation, TIPS owners are guaranteed that their principal would not fall any lower than their original investment.

UPSIDE

In addition to their safety and inflation protection, TIPS offer several other excellent benefits:

• **Tax savings.** Earnings are exempt from state and local taxes.

- **Noncallable**. TIPS are not callable, which means the Treasury cannot redeem them before maturity—unlike bonds issued by many corporations and municipalities.

- **Liquidity.** You can sell TIPS on the secondary market. If you don't want to hold them through maturity, it's easy to find a buyer.

- **Easy to buy.** TIPS are easy to buy and can be purchased through your bank, your broker, or the U.S. Treasury.

DOWNSIDE

The downside to TIPS is that they pay a fairly low interest rate compared with corporate bonds and U.S. Treasury bonds. But the inflation-protection feature eliminates some of the concern you would normally have with fixed-income investments. With other bonds, bond values drop as interest rates rise. But with TIPS, your semiannual interest payment can increase significantly during the term of the bond. Rising inflation and rising interest rates often go together, so as market interest rates rise, there is a good chance that your TIPS returns would increase, as well.

HOW TO BUY TIPS

Like other Treasury securities, TIPS are available in denominations of $1000 and up, with terms of 10 years or 30 years. You can purchase TIPS through a bank, a broker, or—for those who prefer to pay no commission—directly from the U.S. Treasury. To buy from the Treasury, you would go directly through a Federal Reserve branch or the Bureau of Public Debt (1300 C St., S.W., Washington, DC 20239).

In order to buy directly from the Fed, you need to put in a "noncompetitive bid" at a the Treasury's quarterly auction (they occur in February, May, August, and November), which means you are willing to pay the average rate for the securities you want. Otherwise you can buy a Treasury security through a regular bank or brokerage firm for a fee of about $50. They can also be bought and sold on the secondary bond market.

You can also buy TIPS through the U.S. Treasury's Web site, *www.treasurydirect.gov*. You can go to the site, click on the section for "Treasury

Bills, Notes and Bonds," and follow the instructions. You'll be able to buy TIPS online, directly from the U.S. Treasury without paying a commission.

BIGGEST CONCERNS

TIPS are very simple, predictable investments. Because they are adjusted for inflation, you don't have to worry about inflation drain, and because they are backed by the federal government, there's no concern about loss of capital investment. The biggest concern would be deflation. In a period of deflation, the return could decline, although the principal is guaranteed not to drop below the initial par value of the investment. In other words, you have almost nothing to worry about with TIPS.

TIMING

The best time to buy TIPS would be during a period of rising inflation. Because the principal and interest payment rises as inflation rises, TIPS would be more alluring during periods of high inflation than traditional fixed-rate securities, which pay the same interest rate through maturity— which can be for up to 30 years.

By contrast, the worst time to buy TIPS is when inflation is low because your rate of return would be fairly low relative to other fixed-income investments. In the unlikely event of deflation, your TIPS principal could decline, although it could drop no lower than the original par value of the TIPS.

MONITORING YOUR TIPS

It is not easy to find information about TIPS rates and prices, but you can find up-to-date information at the U.S. Treasury Web site, *www.treasury-direct.gov* or at *www.publicdebt.treas.gov*. You'll also be kept up-to-date on the size of your inflation-adjusted principal and your interest payment in the statement that comes with your semiannual interest check.

ASSET ALLOCATION

The amount of money you allocate toward TIPS would depend on your tax situation, your financial situation, your investment goals, and your threshold for risk.

Conservative investors who are more concerned with preservation of spending power than they are with growth might want to invest 20 to 60 percent of their assets in TIPS or a combination of TIPS and T-Bonds or notes under normal economic conditions. You might want to lighten the weighting of Treasuries in the portfolio during periods of low interest rates, and increase the weighting during periods of high interest.

Aggressive investors looking for long-term growth would probably want to limit their investment in TIPS, particularly in times of low inflation. However, an allocation of 5 to 20 percent of assets in TIPS or other Treasury securities even for aggressive investors would help provide balance and diversification, and could buoy the portfolio when stocks are down.

SPECIAL CONSIDERATIONS

One of the great benefits of TIPS is that their value or principal increases in step with inflation. But that can complicate your tax situation. Every time the principal increases, that's considered a taxable gain. Although the bonds are exempt from state and local taxes, those gains are subject to federal income taxes. If your principal increases, you are subject to taxes on those gains each year—even though you wouldn't receive the gains from your inflation-adjusted principal until the security matures.

U.S. TREASURY BILLS

Safety and Low, Short-Term Income

KNOWN AS *T-BILLS*, Treasury Bills are geared entirely to short-term investors. They have the shortest maturity of all Treasury issues, with terms of 4 weeks, 13 weeks, and 26 weeks.

T-bills are similar to U.S. Savings bonds in that investors pay less than the face amount to buy the bills, but receive the full face amount when the bill matures. For instance, you might pay $9500 for a $10,000 T-bill, and receive the full $10,000 when the bill matures. T-bills are issued in minimum denominations of $10,000 and in $5000 increments above $10,000.

Like all U.S. Treasury debt securities, T-bills are considered to be virtually immune from default because they are backed by the full faith and credit of the U.S. government. They are also exempt from state and local taxes. However, as with T-bonds and T-notes, earnings from T-bills is still subject to federal income taxes.

T-bills are designed strictly for short-term investors and have no place in a long-term portfolio. Their strength is their safety and liquidity, but you pay dearly for those benefits. T-bills are the lowest yielding of all Treasury securities. Their yields in recent years have hovered around 1 percent—which doesn't even equal the rate of inflation. For the typical individual investor, money in the bank or a certificate of deposit would make more sense than buying T-bills.

WHO SHOULD BUY TREASURY BILLS?

T-bills are purchased primarily by banks, corporations, and institutional investors to garner a small return on their short-term assets. If you want absolute safety and a slight break on your taxes in a short-term investment, you might consider T-bills.

WHO SHOULD *NOT* BUY TREASURY BILLS?

T-bills have no place in a long-term investment portfolio. Even for short-term individual investors, T-bills are probably not worth the trouble. You can do as well or better in a bank money market account, a certificate of deposit, or, in some cases, even a standard passbook savings account.

RETURN

T-bills are the lowest yielding Treasury security. With an average annual return since 1925 of 3.8 percent, they trail T-bonds (5.3 percent), AAA-rated corporate bonds (5.8 percent), blue chip stocks (10.7 percent), and even tax-exempt municipal bonds (4.2 percent).

As with bonds and notes, returns for T-bills can vary dramatically from year to year. They offered rates approaching double digits in the 1980s, but in recent years their yields have fallen to about 1 percent.

Figures 7-1 and 7-2 illustrate the comparison between T-bills, long-term T-bonds, and blue chip stocks.

RISKS

There are almost no risks associated with owning T-bills. Like all government-issued debt instruments, they are almost as safe as cash itself because they are backed by the full faith and credit of the federal government.

UPSIDE

There are several benefits of owning T-bills. Safety is the main one, but there are some other benefits, as well, such as:

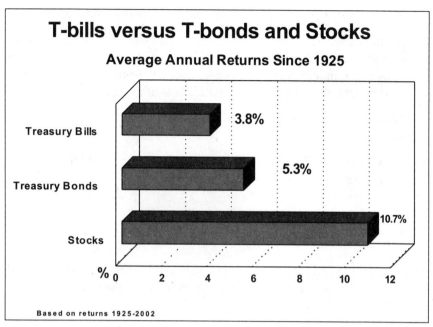

FIGURE 7-1

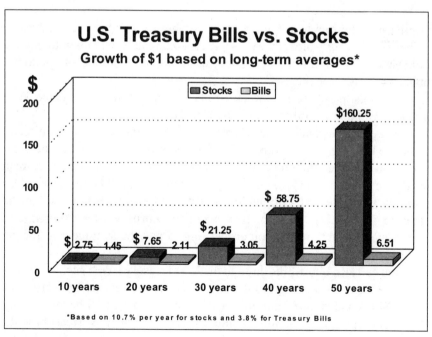

FIGURE 7-2

- **Tax savings.** Earnings are exempt from state and local taxes.

- **Noncallable.** T-bills are not callable, which means the Treasury cannot redeem them before maturity—unlike bonds issued by many corporations and municipalities. Of course, because T-bills are all short-term instruments, the noncallable feature is less of an advantage.

- **Liquidity.** The short-term nature of T-bills means you won't have to wait long to cash them out.

- **Easy to buy.** T-bills are easy to buy and can be purchased through your bank, your broker, or the U.S. Treasury.

DOWNSIDE

The downside to T-bills is that they pay a very low interest rate compared with other types of bonds. In fact, they may not even match the rate of inflation.

HOW TO BUY TREASURY BILLS

T-bills may be purchased for $10,000 or higher in multiples of $5000. When purchasing T-bills, investors pay less than the face amount to buy the bills, but receive the full face amount when the bill matures. T-bills do not make interest payments.

You must purchase four-week T-bills through a broker or a bank. They are not available directly through the U.S. Treasury.

However, you can purchase three-month and six-month T-bills directly from the U.S. Treasury—or through a bank or broker. To buy from the Treasury, you would go directly through a Federal Reserve branch or the Bureau of Public Debt (1300 C St., S.W., Washington, DC 20239). In order to buy directly from the Fed, you need to put in a "noncompetitive bid" at the Treasury's quarterly auction (they occur in February, May, August, and November), which means you are willing to pay the average rate for the securities you want.

You can also buy T-bills through the U.S. Treasury's Web site, *www.treasurydirect.gov*. You can go to the site, click on the section for "Treasury Bills, Notes and Bonds," and follow the instructions. You'll be able to buy T-bills (except four-week bills) online, directly from the U.S. Treasury without paying a commission.

BIGGEST CONCERNS

T-bills are very predictable. When you buy a six-month $10,000 T-bill, you know that in six months, you will collect the full $10,000, no more, no less. You also know you will be earning one of the lowest rates in the fixed-rate market.

The biggest concern might be that if T-bill rates are lower than the rate of inflation, your wealth in real dollar terms would go down every time you cash out another T-bill.

TIMING

The only time to buy T-bills is when you have some money you need to stash in a safe place for a short period of time. They are not appropriate for a long-term portfolio.

MONITORING YOUR TREASURIES

Because of the short-term nature of T-bills, you don't really need to monitor your T-bills. But if you want to find more information on T-bill rates, you can find that at *www.federalreserve.gov* or *www.treasurydirect.gov*. Yield data and other information for Treasury issues is also listed at a number of other Web sites, including *www.investinginbonds.com, www.bondsonline.com*, and *www.forecasts.org*.

ASSET ALLOCATION

There is no point allocating any of your long-term investment assets to T-bills. If you are interested in interest-based investments, there are a number of better options available.

SPECIAL CONSIDERATIONS

Why put your money in T-bills when your bank can give you a rate that is as good or better and save you the trouble of buying and holding T-bills?

STRIPS AND OTHER ZERO-COUPON BONDS

Safety and Capital Appreciation

Z **ERO-COUPON BONDS** are bonds that pay no interest, but rather are issued at a deep discount to face value and gradually increase in value. When the bonds reach maturity, bondholders receive the full face value of the bond.

The most popular type of zeros are known as *STRIPS* (separate trading of registered interest and principal of securities) that originate from Treasury issues, such as T-bonds and T-notes. A number of corporations also offer zero-coupon bonds, and those come with a higher return than Treasury-based bonds, but they don't have the same level of safety.

One of the benefits of zero-coupon bonds is that investors know exactly how much money they will receive when the bond matures. They also know when they will receive the money. And because there are no regular interest payments, they don't have to worry about reinvesting the small payments that normally come from regular bonds.

In a nutshell, zeros are simply bonds that have been stripped of their regular interest payments and repackaged. Historically, most bonds had coupons attached to them that investors would use to redeem their semiannual interest payment. Some investment companies began "stripping" the coupons from the bonds and selling the bonds without the redeemable coupons. Thus the term "zero coupon." When a bond is stripped, each interest payment and the principal payment becomes a separate zero-coupon security. When you buy a zero-coupon bond, it comes without "coupons"—regular interest payments—but rather pays you a set amount at maturity that is equal to the sum of the principal and compounded interest payments that the bond would have paid.

You can use zeros for your long-term investment portfolio, or you can use them to plan ahead for anticipated needs, such as college tuition for the kids, because zeros have a specific schedule of appreciation. You know exactly when you will receive the lump sum payment for your bond and exactly what that payment will be.

WHO SHOULD BUY ZERO-COUPON BONDS?

STRIPS and other zero coupons are geared to investors who want to receive a preset payment at a specific future date. Some pension funds invest in STRIPS to be sure they have adequate funds to cover future payments. Zeros are also popular with investors who buy them for their retirement accounts, 401(k)-type savings plans, and other income tax-advantaged accounts that permit earnings to accumulate without incurring immediate income tax charges.

Zeros are also popular with investors who are saving for a specific future expense, such as college costs for the kids. They are also popular with investors on a limited budget because many zero-coupon bonds are issued in small denominations of under $1000.

Conservative investors who do not need income but want safety, capital appreciation, and some tax savings may find STRIPS alluring. Other zero-coupon bonds derived from higher yielding corporate bonds may be attractive to more aggressive investors. Although zeros from corporate bonds offer neither the safety nor the state and local tax exemption that STRIPS provide, they do offer a better total rate of return.

WHO SHOULD *NOT* BUY ZERO-COUPON BONDS?

If you need current income, STRIPS and other types of zero-coupon bonds would not be for you.

STRIPS would probably not be appropriate for aggressive investors looking for a high rate of return, although aggressive investors may find some corporate zeros that would provide a suitable return. STRIPS and other zeros may also be appropriate (in moderation) for the portfolios of nearly any type of investor interested in diversification.

RETURN

The return from zero-coupon bonds is about the same as any other bond— the difference is that the gains come at the end when the bond matures instead of in regular payments throughout the term of the bond. T-bonds have had an average annual return of about 5.3 percent since 1925, which is somewhat higher than the shorter-term T-notes. Triple-A corporate bonds have averaged about 5.8 percent since 1925, while high yield (junk) bonds offer yields of 2 to 4 points higher than the blue chip bonds. By comparison, blue chip stocks have averaged about 10.7 percent per year since 1925.

Bond returns can vary greatly from year to year. Returns for T-bonds and T-notes hit double-digits in the early 1980s—as high as 14 percent— but dropped to less than 5 percent in 2003. In 2003, while T-bonds were paying about 4.9 percent, 10-year notes were paying only about 3.9 percent. The shorter the maturity, the lower the yield. Seven-year notes were paying 3.44 percent, five-year notes were at 2.85 percent, three-year notes were at 1.87 percent, and two-year notes were at just 1.56 percent.

RISKS

Zero-coupon bonds carry risks similar to the bonds from which they originate. STRIPS are as safe as any other Treasury security, which are considered among the safest of all investments because they are backed by the full faith and credit of the U.S. government. On the other hand, zeros from AAA corporate bonds would be considered very safe, but not as safe as STRIPS, while zeros from junk bonds would be considered the riskiest of all zero-coupon bonds.

Market prices of zero-coupon bonds can fluctuate more than the prices of traditional bonds with the same maturity because the market price reflects the fact that there is only one payment for zeros, which is to be made well into the future. By contrast, traditional bondholders have a little more certainty with their returns because they receive a steady stream of interest payments throughout the life of the bond. The longer the maturity of a zero-coupon bond, the greater the potential for market price fluctuation.

UPSIDE

Zero-coupon bonds can offer several solid benefits:

- **No interest payments**. Rather than receive a series of small interest payments that you may need to reinvest, zeros pay you one lump sum upon maturity.

- **Easy to buy**. Zero-coupon bonds are readily available through many banks and brokers.

- **Liquidity**. You can resell your zero-coupon bonds on the secondary market through a broker.

- **Tax benefits for STRIPS**. Gains from Treasury STRIPS are exempt from state and local taxes.

- **Safety for STRIPS**. STRIPS are very safe because they are backed by the U.S. government, although other types of zeros not backed by the government do not offer that same level of safety.

- **STRIPS are noncallable.** All Treasury securities are noncallable, which means they cannot be redeemed by the government before maturity—unlike many bonds issued by corporations and municipalities. Sometimes when market interest rates start to fall, some corporations and municipalities pay off their bonds early and reissue new bonds at the lower rate. That would not happen with STRIPS because they are noncallable.

DOWNSIDE

Even though STRIPS and other zero-coupon bonds pay no interest, you are still liable for taxes on the annual gains in the value of the bonds. So you must pay taxes on gains that you have not yet received.

Like other government securities, STRIPS pay a fairly low return compared with many other types of investments. But zero-coupon corporate bonds can offer a little better bang for your buck.

HOW TO BUY STRIPS AND OTHER ZERO-COUPON BONDS

STRIPS and other zero-coupon bonds are available only through banks and brokers. You cannot buy STRIPS directly from the Treasury as you can with other Treasury securities because the original bonds are purchased by brokerage companies and "stripped" of their income component (known as the "coupon") before they are repackaged into zero-coupon bonds. When a bond is stripped, each interest payment and the principal payment becomes a separate zero-coupon security.

zero-coupon bonds are available in a wide range of denominations, from a few hundred dollars to tens of thousands of dollars.

When you buy zeros, you pay less than face value, and when you redeem them years later, you receive the full face value. For example, if you bought a 10-year STRIPS with a $1000 face value, you would pay about $527. That balance would grow steadily at a 6.5 percent rate. After 10 years, you would receive a $1000 principal payment, which would include your $527 initial investment along with $483 in interest accrued over the 10-year life of the bond.

You pay no commission to purchase zero-coupon bonds from brokers, but the sale price will include a markup that the broker pockets.

BIGGEST CONCERNS

STRIPS are very predictable investments and very safe because they are based on bonds issued by the U.S. government. When the STRIPS matures, you will receive the full par value.

However, zero-coupon bonds based on other types of bonds, such as municipal and corporate bonds, carry a higher risk of default. Worst-case scenario, you could lose your entire investment if the bond issuer defaults. That is not likely to happen with A-grade corporate bonds, but it has happened on rare occasions with junk bonds and municipal bonds, so there is some risk factor.

The other concern is that if you buy long-term zeros during periods of low interest rates, you could see a rise in rates, leaving you with one of the lowest-yielding bonds on the market. But if you tried to sell your bond to reinvest at a higher rate, you would have to sell it at a discount because bond values decline as market interest rates rise.

TIMING

The best time to buy STRIPS and other zero-coupon bonds, as with near-ly all traditional types of bonds, would be during periods of high interest rates. It can be difficult to predict the movement of interest rates, but as interest rates drop, the value of existing bonds increases. Buying a fixed-rate investment near the peak of interest rates would put you in a very strong position. As interest rates drop, you could hold the bond and con-tinue to enjoy high returns, or you could sell the bond at a premium, earn-ing a tidy profit on your investment.

By contrast, the worst time to buy zeros would be during a period when interest rates are low and are beginning to rise. That would put you in the unenviable position of either earning low rates throughout the term of the bond or selling it out at a loss. You could opt for bonds with shorter terms, but the shorter the term, the worse the return. When rates are low, your options are all less than ideal.

MONITORING YOUR ZEROS

STRIPS investors receive a report each year from their financial institution displaying the amount of STRIPS interest income they earned for that year. This statement is known as "IRS Form 1099—OID," the acronym for orig-inal issue discount. You would receive a similar statement from the issuers of other types of zero-coupon bonds to help you keep track of your bond's status.

You can also find current bond rates and other information about bonds and STRIPS at the federal government's own Web site—*www.treasury direct.gov*. Yield data and other information is also listed for bonds and other zero-coupon bonds at a number of other Web sites, including *www.investing-inbonds.com*, *www.bondsonline.com*, and *www.forecasts.org*.

ASSET ALLOCATION

If you need income from your investments, zero-coupon bonds are probably not right for you. But if you are investing for long-term capital appreciation, zero-coupon bonds may have a place in your portfolio. As with all types of investments, asset allocation depends on your own goals and threshold for risk.

Conservative investors who are more concerned with preservation of capital than they are with income might want to invest 20 to 60 percent of their assets in zero coupons and other types of bonds, such as T-bonds, T-notes, and corporate bonds. You might want to lighten the weighting of zeros and other fixed-rate investments during periods of low interest rates, and increase the weighting during periods of high interest.

If you are saving for a specific purpose, such as college education expenses, you may want to put a little more of your money into zero-coupon bonds that will mature when your college expenses begin.

Aggressive investors looking for long-term growth would probably want to limit their investment in zeros, particularly in times of low interest. However, an allocation of 5 to 20 percent of assets in STRIPS, zeros, and other bonds and notes, even for aggressive investors, would help provide balance and diversification, and could buoy the portfolio when stocks are down.

SPECIAL CONSIDERATIONS

If you buy zero-coupon bonds for your investment portfolio, you might want to consider buying them primarily for your tax-advantaged retirement fund (IRA, SEP, or 401k). Otherwise you are subject to income taxes on your gains each year, even though you would not receive any money until the bond matures.

9

MUNICIPAL BONDS

Tax-Exempt Income

I F YOU LIKE STEADY INCOME but you don't like taxes, municipal bonds could be just the ticket. Municipal bonds—"munis" for short—are issued by state and local government entities in order to raise money for projects, operations, and capital expenditures.

The biggest allure of municipal bonds is that the interest income they pay is exempt from federal taxes, and in some cases, it's also exempt from state and local taxes for residents of the state in which the bond is issued.

Munis come in two basic types, revenue bonds and general obligation bonds. Revenue bonds are used by state and local government entities to raise money for projects such as schools, roads, stadiums, and water and sewer projects. General obligation bonds are used to finance municipal or state operations and capital expenditures.

Municipal bonds are offered in denominations of as little as $1000, although a $10,000 minimum is more common. You buy municipal bonds at face value, collect your tax-exempt interest throughout the term of the bond, and receive your principal back in full when the bond matures.

In addition to the tax benefits of munis, they are also considered to be very safe investments. They are not quite as safe as U.S. Treasury securities because they are not backed by the federal government. But of the thousands of different municipal bonds issued in the past decade or so, only a handful have defaulted.

The drawback to municipal bonds is that they pay a fairly low yield. But because of their tax advantages, their yield is not a true reflection of the after-tax return. For instance, for an investor in the 31-percent tax bracket, a 4-percent tax-exempt bond would provide nearly the same after-tax return as a taxable 6-percent bond.

Table 9-1 shows the comparative after-tax yield of munis versus taxable bonds at various interest rate levels. The higher the tax bracket, the more you would have to earn in a taxable bond to receive the same after-tax return as a muni.

TABLE 9-1 *Equivalent After-tax Return of a Tax-exempt versus a Taxable Bond*

TAX-EXEMPT RETURN	15% TAX BRACKET	28% TAX BRACKET	31% TAX BRACKET
4% =	4.7% taxable	5.5% taxable	5.8% taxable
5% =	5.88	6.94	7.25
6% =	7.05	8.33	8.7
7% =	8.23	9.72	10.14
8% =	9.41	11.11	11.59

Municipal bonds are not for every investor. But for conservative investors in search of tax-free income, they're an ideal choice.

WHO SHOULD BUY MUNICIPAL BONDS?

Munis are most attractive to investors looking for tax-exempt income. They are very popular with affluent, conservative investors. About 5 million Americans hold municipal bonds in some form, whether it's an individual bond, a bond mutual fund, or a unit investment trust.

WHO SHOULD *NOT* BUY MUNICIPAL BONDS?

Munis are not appropriate for investors interested in capital appreciation, nor would they be appropriate for aggressive investors looking for a high total return.

Municipal bonds would definitely not be suitable for tax-favored retirement accounts, such as IRAs, SEPs, and 401k plans. The tax exemption that munis provide would be lost in a tax-advantaged retirement plan. Among fixed-income investments, you would be better served to use higher-yielding taxable bonds for a tax-advantaged retirement account.

RETURN

Municipal bonds pay a lower rate of return than most other types of bonds, including T-bonds, T-bills, and corporate bonds. However, because of their tax-favored status, the relative after-tax return municipal bonds offer would still be nearly as good as—if not better than—many other bonds (depending on your tax bracket). High-quality municipal bonds yield about 15 percent less than comparable government securities, so if you're in the 15-percent tax bracket, or higher, your relative return with munis could be as high as T-bonds and T-notes (or higher, depending on your state tax status).

As with most types of bonds, interest rates for municipal bonds can vary greatly from year to year. Since 1925, municipal bonds have provided an average annual return of about 4.2 percent, compared with a average return of 5.3 percent for T-bonds, 5.8 percent for corporate bonds, and 10.7 percent for stocks.

Generally speaking, the longer the term of the municipal bond, the higher the return you would receive. For instance, 30-year municipal bonds were recently paying about 5.3 percent, while 10-year munis were around 4.2 percent.

Figures 9-1 and 9-2 illustrate the comparison between municipal bonds and blue chip stocks.

RISKS

Municipal bonds are considered very safe, but not as safe as U.S. Treasury securities, such as T-bonds, T-notes, and T-bills. Munis have been known to default on rare occasions. To play it safe, you should have a diversified selection of municipal bonds in your portfolio. Some advisors suggest that you may need $100,000 or more in munis to create a properly diversified muni portfolio.

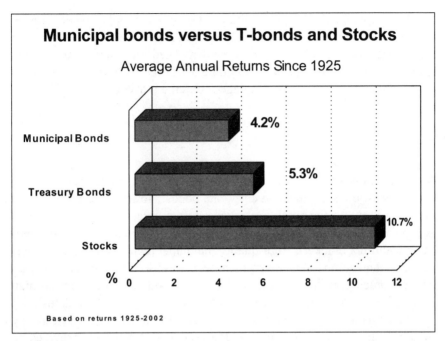

FIGURE 9-1

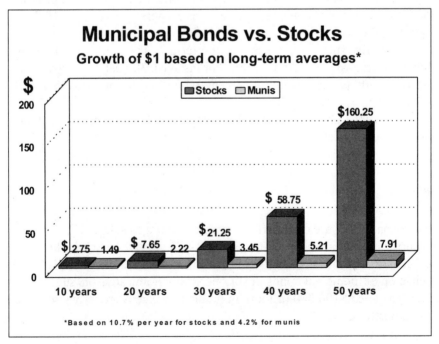

FIGURE 9-2

If that sounds like more than you can afford, there are two other ways to lower your risk. You could buy a municipal bond mutual fund. There are a number of specialized funds available from some of the leading mutual fund companies. (For bond rankings and other research to help you find a good fund, you can check out the periodic rankings in a number of publications, including *Money*, *Consumer Reports*, and *Baron's*. There are also some good sites online that include mutual fund information, including *AllstarStocks.com*, *America Online*, *morningstar.com*, and *multexinvestor.com*.)

The other option is to buy insured munis. You cannot actually buy insurance on your individual bonds, but you can buy bonds that already have insurance attached to them. About half of the bonds issued now have insurance available, but it does cut slightly into your return. Bond insurers guarantee bondholders that they will receive timely payment of interest and principal throughout the term of the bond.

UPSIDE

Clearly the tax-exempt status of municipal bonds is their biggest and most important benefit. But there are several other important benefits, such as:

- **Safety.** Although they are not as safe as Treasury securities, municipal bonds are considered to be relatively safe investments.
- **Income.** Munis provide a steady stream of tax-exempt income.
- **Liquidity.** Municipal bonds can be bought and sold on the secondary market, giving investors an opportunity to unload their bonds if they need to cash out early.
- **Easy to buy.** Munis are easy to buy and can be purchased through your bank or your broker.

DOWNSIDE

Municipal bond rates are not especially enticing, so they are not likely to show up in the portfolios of most aggressive investors.

Another drawback of munis is that most of them are callable, so they can be redeemed early. If you're shopping for a municipal bond, find out how many years of call protection you'll receive. One more concern for muni owners is that the secondary market for some bonds is very thin, so you may have a little trouble selling out if you want to dump your bond early.

HOW TO BUY MUNICIPAL BONDS

Municipal bonds come in denominations of as little as $1000, although a $10,000 minimum is more common. You can purchase municipal bonds through banks and brokerage firms.

Although billions of dollars of municipal bonds are on the market, there is no centralized marketplace that trades munis as there is for stocks. Instead, they are bought and sold by many banks and brokerage firms that specialize in municipal bonds. About 2700 securities dealers (banks and brokerage firms) throughout the country are registered with the Municipal Securities Rulemaking Board (MSRB) in Washington, D.C. to buy and sell municipal bonds. To buy a muni, you must use a broker or banker who is tied into this specialized network.

As with most other types of bonds, brokers generally do not charge a separate commission to buy or sell municipal bonds. They make their money by imposing a small markup. Transaction costs on municipal bonds compare favorably with those on other securities. When you buy a bond in the secondary market, you would pay an extra 0.5 to 3 percent, depending on the size of the bond and some other factors. For small lots or lower-rated bonds, the broker markup could be 3 to 4 percent.

BIGGEST CONCERNS

Not all municipal bonds are able to maintain their tax-exempt status through the life of the bond. The IRS has gotten tougher on munis, and can now tax muni investors when it finds that the bonds don't comply with tax laws and it can't reach a settlement with the issuer. While most bonds will continue to maintain a tax-exempt status, that is no longer guaranteed.

TIMING

Like most bonds, the best time to buy municipal bonds would be during periods of high interest rates. As interest rates drop, the value of existing bonds increases. Buying bonds near the peak of interest rates would put you in a strong position. As interest rates drop, you could hold the bond and continue to enjoy high returns, or you could sell the bond at a premium, earning a tidy profit on your investment.

By contrast, the worst time to buy munis would be during a period when interest rates are low and are beginning to rise. That would put you in the position of either collecting low rates throughout the term of the bond, or selling it out at a loss. You could opt for bonds with shorter terms, but the shorter the term, the worse the return. When rates are low, if you need income, you may not have much choice but to buy more bonds, but it's a much better option to buy bonds when interest rates are high.

MONITORING YOUR MUNIS

There are more than 2 million different municipal bond issues outstanding. There is no publication or Web site that can keep you up-to-date on all 2 million bonds. That would take too much effort and too much space. If you have questions on your bond, you should direct them to the banker or broker who sold you the bond.

You can find prices for some of the most actively traded muni bonds in the financial press, such as *The Wall Street Journal* and *Investors' Business Daily*. You also might find yield data and other information on some of the bonds at a number of Web sites, including *www.investinginbonds.com*, *www.bondsonline.com*, and *www.forecasts.org*. Daily price and yield information for more than 1000 actively traded munis is available at *investinginbonds.com*, which is the Web site of the Bond Market Association. The site also provides a daily update on benchmark yields provided by The Bond Market Association/Bloomberg National Municipal Yields Table. It shows yields of insured revenue bonds with seven different maturities, from 2 to 30 years and includes a comparison with the previous week and six months ago, as well as a taxable equivalent yield.

You can also call 1-800-BOND INFO to get up to 25 transaction prices (or price evaluations for bonds that haven't traded recently) for a modest cost. The service, known as Standard & Poor's/The Bond Market Association Municipal Bond Service, is designed for individual investors who want to monitor changes or get updates on their bond holdings.

ASSET ALLOCATION

Studies have shown that munis have a low correlation with stocks, which makes them a good investment to balance out your stock portfolio. But the amount of money you allocate toward munis would depend on your tax situation, your financial situation, your investment goals, and your threshold for risk. The higher your tax income bracket, the more attractive munis become.

Conservative investors who are more concerned with preservation of capital than they are with growth might want to invest 20 to 60 percent of their assets in municipal bonds and other types of bonds and fixed-income investments under normal economic conditions. You might want to lighten the weighting during periods of low interest rates, and increase the weighting during periods of high interest.

Aggressive investors looking for long-term growth would probably want to limit their investment in munis, particularly in times of low interest. However, an allocation of 5 to 20 percent of assets in bonds of some type even for aggressive investors can help provide balance and diversification, and could buoy the portfolio when stocks are down.

SPECIAL CONSIDERATIONS

The best way to judge the safety of any particular issue is to look at the bond's safety rating by one of the leading bond rating services, such as Standard & Poor's, Moody's, or Fitch.

Municipal bonds are priced based on their credit quality, maturity, liquidity, and yield. According to the Bond Market Association, yield is the most important element for an investor in evaluating the merits of a transaction as well as comparing costs of alternatives. The municipal bond market is a dealer market, and bond dealers compete with each other for customers on the basis of yield and other factors. Bond dealers price their bonds at a yield that is based on several factors, including:

- Prevailing interest rates in the market

- Supply and demand for the bond

- Creditworthiness of the issuer

- Maturity term

- Call provisions

- Track record of the issuer

- Trading volume of the bonds, and

- Level of difficulty in finding a buyer

If you find a bond that has a much higher yield than most other bonds on the market, there may be a good reason for that. It may be that the issuer has credit problems, or that there is no demand for the bond. Or it could be that the bond is likely to be called early by the issuer. That's why it is important to check out a bond thoroughly before you invest. Before you buy a bond, ask your broker how the bond stacks up on all of those key factors listed above.

10

MUNI ZEROS (ZERO-COUPON MUNICIPAL BONDS)

Tax-Exempt Capital Appreciation

ZERO-COUPON MUNICIPAL BONDS take the guesswork and suspense out of investing. When you buy a 10-year muni zero, you know exactly how much you'll receive—tax-free—10 years from the day you buy it. Muni zeros pay no interest, but rather are issued at a deep discount to face value and gradually increase in value. When the bond reaches maturity, bondholders receive the full face value of the bond.

Like the municipal bonds from which they are derived, zero-coupon munis are exempt from all federal income taxes, and, in many cases are also exempt from state and local taxes for investors who live in the state in which they are issued. So when you buy a 10-year, $10,000 zero-coupon municipal bond, you know that 10 years from now when the bond matures you will receive $10,000, no strings attached.

In addition to the tax benefits of munis, they are also considered to be very safe investments. They are not quite as safe as U.S. Treasury securities, which are backed by the federal government. But of the hundreds of thousands of municipal bonds issued in the past decade, only a handful have defaulted.

The drawback to municipal bonds is that they pay a fairly low yield. But because of their tax savings, their yield is not a true reflection of the after-tax return. For instance, for an investor in the 31-percent tax bracket, a 4-percent tax-exempt muni would provide nearly the same after-tax return as a taxable 6-percent bond.

To get the same average annual return as the stock market—which has grown at about 10.7 percent since 1925—you would need a muni zero with about a 7.3-percent yield. So if you owned a 10-year muni zero with a 7.3-percent yield, that would be like hitting the stock market average 10 years in a row—with no volatility, no uncertainty, no buying and selling, and far less risk than the stock market. No wonder municipal zeros have become increasingly popular with American investors!

Figure 10-1 shows how municipal zeros with varying rates would compare in after-tax terms with the average annual stock market return:

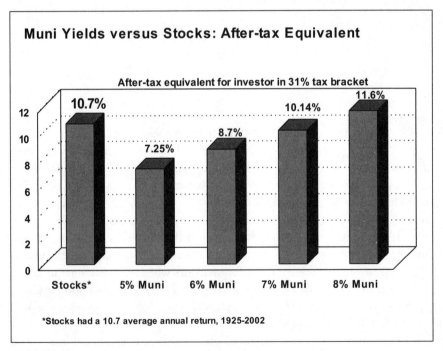

FIGURE 10-1

WHO SHOULD BUY MUNI ZEROS?

Muni zeros are geared to investors who want to receive a preset payment at a specific future date. They are popular with investors who are saving for a specific future expense, such as college costs for the kids.

Conservative, affluent investors who do not need income but want tax savings, capital appreciation, and some safety are often attracted to zero-coupon munis. Municipal bond zeros may also be appropriate (in moderation) for the portfolios of nearly any type of investor interested in diversification.

WHO SHOULD *NOT* BUY MUNI ZEROS?

If you need current income, zero munis are not for you because they pay no income. Nor would muni zeros be appropriate for aggressive investors looking for a high rate of return.

Muni zeros would definitely not be suitable for tax-favored retirement accounts, such as IRAs, SEPs, and 401k plans. The tax exemption that munis provide would be lost in a tax-advantaged retirement plan. If you want a fixed-income investment in your IRA or other tax-advantaged retirement account, you would be better served to use higher-yielding taxable zero-coupon bonds or traditional bonds.

RETURN

The return from municipal zero-coupon bonds is about the same as any other municipal bond—the difference is that the gains come at the end when the bond matures instead of in regular payments throughout the term of the bond.

Municipal bonds generally pay a lower rate of return than most other types of bonds, including T-bonds, T-bills, and corporate bonds. However, because of their tax-favored status, the relative after-tax return muni zeros offer would still be nearly as good as—if not better than—many other bonds (depending on your tax bracket). High-quality municipal bonds yield about 15 percent less than comparable government securities, so if you're in the 15-percent tax bracket, or higher, your relative return with munis could be as high as T-bonds and T-notes (or higher, depending on your state tax status).

Since 1925, municipal bonds have provided an average annual return of about 4.2 percent, compared with a average return of 5.3 percent for T-bonds, 5.8 percent for corporate bonds, and 10.7 percent for stocks.

Generally speaking, the longer the term of the municipal bond, the higher the return you would receive. For instance, 30-year municipal bonds were recently paying about 5.3 percent, while 10-year munis were around 4.2 percent.

RISKS OF MUNI ZEROS

Muni zeros carry risks similar to the bonds from which they were derived. Although a handful of municipal bonds have defaulted in the past decade, municipal bonds are generally considered very safe. To reduce your risk, you can buy insured muni zeros. About half of the municipal bonds issued now have insurance available, but it does cut slightly into your return. Bond insurers guarantee that zero-coupon bondholders will receive the full payment of interest and principal when their bond matures.

Market prices of muni zeros can fluctuate more than the price of traditional municipal bonds with the same maturity because the market price reflects the fact that there is only one payment for a zero-coupon bond, which is to be made well into the future. By contrast, traditional bondholders have a little more certainty with their returns because they receive a steady stream of interest payments throughout the life of the bond. The longer the maturity of a muni zero, the greater the potential for market price fluctuation.

UPSIDE

In addition to their tax-exempt status, muni zeros offer several solid benefits:

- **No interest payments**. Rather than receive a series of small interest payments that you may need to reinvest, zeros pay you one lump sum upon maturity.

- **No periodic tax payments**. With most zero-coupon bonds, you are still liable each year for income taxes on the annual gains in the value of the bonds. As a result, you must pay taxes on gains that you have not yet received. With muni zeros, you would pay no federal tax ever, and, depending on the bond, you might not owe any state or local taxes either.

- **Easy to buy**. Zero-coupon bonds are readily available through many banks and brokers.

- **Liquidity**. You can resell your zero-coupon bonds on the secondary market through a broker, although some thinly traded issues are much harder to sell than others.

- **Safety**. Municipal bonds are considered to be among the safest bonds on the market, although they are not quite as safe as Treasury securities, which are backed by the full faith and credit of the U.S. government.

DOWNSIDE TO MUNI ZEROS

Like other municipal bonds, muni zeros pay a fairly low return compared with many other types of investments.

Another drawback for muni zeros and other municipal bonds is that most of them are callable, so they can be redeemed early. If you're shopping for a muni zero, find out how many years of call protection you'll receive. One more concern for muni owners is that the secondary market for some bonds is very thin, so you may have a little trouble selling out if you want dump your bond early.

HOW TO BUY MUNI ZEROS

Zero-coupon municipal bonds are available only through banks and brokers.

When you buy zeros, you pay less than face value, and when you redeem them years later, you would receive the full face value. For example, if you bought a 10-year muni zero with a $1000 face value, you would pay about $527. That balance would grow steadily at a 6.5 percent rate. After 10 years, you would receive a $1000 principal payment, which would include your $527 initial investment along with $483 in interest accrued over the 10-year life of the bond.

Although billions of dollars of municipal bonds are on the market, there is no centralized marketplace that trades municipal bonds as there is for stocks. Instead, they are bought and sold by many banks and brokerage firms that specialize in municipal bonds. To buy a muni, you must use a broker or banker who is tied into this specialized network.

As with most other types of bonds, brokers generally do not charge a separate commission to buy or sell muni zeros. They make their money by imposing a small markup. Transaction costs on municipal bonds compare favorably with those on other securities. When you buy a bond in the secondary market, you would pay an extra 0.5 to 3 percent, depending on the size of the bond and some other factors. For small lots or lower rated bonds, the broker markup could be 3 to 4 percent.

BIGGEST CONCERNS

Muni zeros are very predictable investments because you know when they will pay off and exactly the amount they will pay. While there is some risk of default with munis, the risk is very low.

The other concern is that if you buy long-term muni zeros during periods of low interest rates, you could see a rise in rates, leaving you with one of the lowest-yielding bonds on the market. But if you tried to sell your bond to reinvest at a higher rate, you would have to sell it at a discount because bond values decline as market interest rates rise.

TIMING

The best time to buy muni zeros, as with nearly all traditional types of bonds, would be during periods of high interest rates. It can be difficult to predict the movement of interest rates, but as interest rates drop, the value of existing bonds increases. Buying a fixed-rate investment near the peak of interest rates would put you in a very strong position. As interest rates drop, you could hold the bond and continue to enjoy high returns, or you could sell the bond at a premium, earning a tidy profit on your investment.

By contrast, the worst time to buy zeros (or other bonds) would be during a period when interest rates are low and are beginning to rise. That would put you in the unenviable position of either earning low rates throughout the term of the bond, or selling it out at a loss. You could opt for bonds with shorter terms, but the shorter the term, the worse the return. When rates are low, your options are all less than ideal.

MONITORING YOUR MUNI ZEROS

With more than 2 million different municipal bond issues outstanding, there is no publication or Web site that can keep you up-to-date on the entire market. If you have questions on your zero-coupon municipal bond, you should direct them to the banker or broker who sold you the bond.

You can find prices for some of the most actively traded muni bonds in the financial press, such as *The Wall Street Journal* and *Investors' Business Daily*. You also might find yield data and other information on some of the bonds at a number of Web sites, including *www.investinginbonds.com*, *www.bondsonline.com*, and *www.forecasts.org*. Daily price and yield information for over 1000 actively traded munis is available at *investinginbonds.com*, which is the Web site of the Bond Market Association. The site also provides a daily update on benchmark yields provided by The Bond Market Association/Bloomberg National Municipal Yields Table. It shows yields of insured revenue bonds with seven different maturities, from 2 to 30 years, and includes a comparison with the previous week and six months ago as well as a taxable equivalent yield.

You can also call 1-800-BOND INFO to get up to 25 transaction prices (or price evaluations for bonds that haven't traded recently) for a modest cost. The service, known as Standard & Poor's/The Bond Market Association Municipal Bond Service, is designed for individual investors who want to monitor changes or get updates on their bond holdings.

ASSET ALLOCATION

If you need income from your investments, muni zeros are probably not right for you. But if you are investing for long-term capital appreciation, they may have a place in your portfolio. Studies have shown that munis have a low correlation with stocks, which makes them a good investment to balance out your stock portfolio. But the amount of money you allocate toward muni zeros would depend on your tax situation, your financial situation, your investment goals, and your threshold for risk. The higher your tax income bracket, the more attractive munis become.

Conservative investors who are more concerned with preservation of capital than they are with income might want to invest 20 to 60 percent of their assets in muni zeros and other types of bonds, such as T-bonds, T-notes, and corporate bonds. You might want to lighten the weighting of zeros and other fixed-rate investments during periods of low interest rates, and increase the weighting during periods of high interest.

If you are saving for a specific purpose, such as college education expenses, you may want to put a little more of your money into muni zeros or other types of zero-coupon bonds that will mature when your college expenses begin.

Aggressive investors looking for long-term growth would probably want to limit their investment in muni zeros, particularly in times of low interest. However, an allocation of 5 to 20 percent of assets in munis and other bonds and notes, even for aggressive investors, would help provide balance and diversification, and could buoy the portfolio when stocks are down.

SPECIAL CONSIDERATIONS FOR MUNI ZEROS

The best way to judge the safety of any particular issue is to look at the bond's safety rating by the leading bond rating services, such as Standard & Poor's, Moody's, or Fitch.

Municipal bonds are priced based on their credit quality, maturity, liquidity, and yield. According to the Bond Market Association, yield is the most important element for an investor in evaluating the merits of a transaction as well as comparing costs of alternatives. The municipal bond market is a dealer market, and bond dealers compete with each other for customers on the basis of yield and other factors. Bond dealers price their bonds at a yield that is based on several factors, including prevailing interest rates in the market, supply and demand for the bond, creditworthiness of the issuer, maturity term, call provisions, track record of the issuer, trading volume of the bonds, and level of difficulty in finding a buyer.

If you find a muni zero that has a much higher yield than most other bonds on the market, there may be a good reason for that. It may be that the issuer has credit problems, or that there is no demand for the bond. Or it could be that the bond is likely to be called early by the issuer. That's why it is important to check out a bond thoroughly before you invest, and to ask your broker how the bond stacks up on all of the key factors listed above.

11

MORTGAGE-BACKED SECURITIES

Good Income, Low Risk

MORTGAGE-BACKED SECURITIES are fixed-income investments that generate interest revenue through pools of home loan mortgages. Sometimes referred to as MBS or "pools" or "mortgage pass-through certificates," mortgage securities are an excellent source of current income. Although they don't have quite the safety of government-backed Treasury issues, mortgage-backed securities are very safe, and they pay interest rates slightly higher than Treasury issues and many investment-grade corporate bonds.

MBS investors own an interest in a pool of mortgages that serve as the underlying asset for the MBS. When homeowners make their monthly payment of interest and a small share of the principal, that money is passed through to the MBS investors or "certificate holders."

Most mortgage-backed securities are issued by three primary agencies: the Government National Mortgage Association (Ginnie Mae), the Federal Home Loan Mortgage Association (Freddie Mac), and the Federal National

Mortgage Association (Fannie Mae). A small number of MBS issues are sold by other lending agencies.

Unlike Treasury issues and municipal bonds, mortgage-backed securities offer no tax benefits. They are fully taxable by state, local, and federal governments. And while Treasury security investors receive interest payments twice a year, MBS investors receive checks every month.

Although home loan mortgage pools are the most common type of MBS, there are other classes of securities similar to mortgage-backed securities but tied to other types of loans. For instance, you might find securities tied to pools of credit card loans, car loans, mobile home loans, college loans, or other types of loans.

In addition to the standard type of MBS, there are several offshoot investments derived from mortgage-backed securities, including:

- CMOs. Collateralized mortgage obligations (CMOs) break up mortgage pools into separate maturity categories called "tranches." Each CMO is a set of two or more tranches, each with average lives and cashflow patterns designed to meet specific investment objectives. One CMO might have four tranches with average life expectancies of 2, 5, 7, and 20 years. That gives investors a wider array of options. Some CMOs have several dozen tranches. The system helps cut back on the early prepayment of mortgages, which is one of the biggest drawbacks of the MBS market. With CMOs, all prepayments from underlying mortgages are applied to the first tranche until it is paid off. Then prepayments are applied to the next tranche until it is paid off, and the process continues until all the tranches are eventually retired. The concept gives investors the ability to choose a tranche that fits their maturity time frame.

- REMICs. Real estate mortgage investments conduits (REMICs) are similar to CMOs with a twist. While CMOs separate mortgage securities into maturity classes, REMICs also separate them into risk classes. A REMIC might have a pool of higher risk or even distressed mortgages, so the risk is higher, but the yield is higher as well. REMICs are the junk bonds of the mortgage-backed securities category.

- STRIPs. Mortgage-backed securities might be stripped of their interest coupons and sold as zero-coupon bonds. Rather than make regular monthly interest and principal payments, STRIPs pay all the principal and compounded interest in one lump sum at maturity.

For investors looking for a steady stream of income at a higher interest rate than most government bonds pay, mortgage-backed securities provide an appealing option.

WHO SHOULD BUY MORTGAGE-BACKED SECURITIES?

Mortgage-backed securities are ideal for investors interested in safety and income. More aggressive investors might also want an MBS for the portfolio to provide diversification. MBSs offer no tax benefits, so they would be appropriate for tax-sheltered retirement plans.

WHO SHOULD *NOT* BUY MBSS?

Mortgage-backed securities would not be appropriate for investors interested in capital appreciation—unless you buy zero-coupon securities. Aggressive investors looking for a high level of income might also shy away from MBSs, although they are among the higher-yielding types of fixed income investments.

RETURN

The return offered by mortgage-backed securities is among the best of all fixed-rate investments. They typically pay a higher return than other government bonds, such as T-bonds and T-notes. In fact, they usually offer rates slightly better than investment-grade corporate bonds.

Although rates can vary depending on the circumstances, as a general rule of thumb, a Ginnie Mae MBS pays a yield of about 1 to 2 percentage points higher than a Treasury issue with the same maturity.

An MBS from Fannie Mae or Freddie Mac pays even more, since they are considered slightly riskier than a Ginnie Mae MBS. They pay a yield of about 15 to 50 basis points percent higher than a Ginnie Mae MBS (100 basis points equals one percentage point). However, the average annual total return from mortgage-backed securities still falls several percentage points below the 10.7-percent average annual return of the stock market. But mortgage-backed securities are much safer and more predictable than stocks.

Unlike most bonds, which make payments twice a year, MBSs provide payments of interest and a small part of the principal every month.

RISKS

Mortgage-backed securities are considered very safe. They are guaranteed by the issuer, and because they are made up of pools of mortgages, their return is not based on a single mortgage holder.

Ginnie Mae securities are technically the safest of all MBS options because they are guaranteed by Ginnie Mae, which is a wholly owned government corporation backed by the full faith and credit of the United States.

Securities issued by Fannie Mae and Freddie Mac are also guaranteed, but not by the full faith and credit of the U.S. government. Fannie Mae and Freddie Mac are publicly traded corporations (you can buy stock in either company on the New York Stock Exchange) originally set up by the U.S. Congress. They guarantee the timely payment of all principal and interest of the mortgage-backed securities they issue. Although their guarantee doesn't carry the weight of the U.S. government, Freddie Mac and Fannie Mae are two of the most fiscally sound corporations in America. Their mortgage-backed securities are considered to be the equivalent of AAA-rated corporate bonds. They have never defaulted on a mortgage-backed security.

UPSIDE

There are several important benefits of owning mortgage-backed securities. Safety and a steady stream of income are the most obvious, but there are some other benefits, as well, such as:

- **Excellent interest rates.** The interest they pay is higher than the rate offered by other government bonds and most investment grade corporate bonds.

- **Liquidity.** There is a huge secondary market for mortgage-backed securities, so you can buy and sell them whenever you wish. If you don't want to hold them through maturity, it's easy to find a buyer on the secondary market.

- **Easy to buy.** They are easy to buy and can be purchased through your bank or your broker.

- **Safety.** Because of the guarantees that come with mortgage-backed securities, they are considered very safe investments.

DOWNSIDE

Perhaps the biggest drawback to mortgage-backed securities is the uncertainty over how long they will continue to pay off. If you buy an MBS when interest rates are high, you might hope to enjoy a great return for the full 30-year term of the security. Unfortunately, if interest rates start to drop, you might be disappointed. Homeowners are very likely to pay off their mortgages when interest rates start falling in order to refinance at a lower rate. So before long, all of the mortgage-buyers in the pool will have refinanced and returned the principal. As a MBS owner, you would receive your principal back, and therefore, would no longer receive interest payments at that high-interest-rate-level. You would need to reinvest your money at a lower rate.

The flip side can be just as frustrating for investors. If you buy an MBS when interest rates are low, if rates start to climb, homeowners are going to hold onto their old mortgages for dear life. Why refinance if you would have to pay a higher rate. As a result, MBS investors would be tied to those low rates for the full term of the security—unable to reinvest their money in the newer, higher-yielding investments.

Mortgage-backed securities have some other minor drawbacks, as well:

- **Lower return than stocks.** Although mortgage-backed securities typically pay higher rates than other government bonds and AAA corporate bonds, they still fall well below average annual returns offered by stocks and high-yield corporate bonds. But they are much safer than stocks or junk bonds.

- **Long terms.** Many mortgage-backed securities are issued with terms of up to 30 years, so you could be stuck with them for a long time. However, you can buy an MBS with a shorter term on the secondary market, and you can unload your MBS on the secondary market whenever you wish.

- **High cost of admission.** If you want to buy a MBS from Ginnie Mae, the lowest-priced security you can purchase is $25,000. However, Freddie Mac and Fannie Mae securities are available in $1000 increments.

- **Fully taxable.** Unlike government bonds, mortgage-backed securities are fully taxable by federal, state, and local governments.

HOW TO BUY MORTGAGE-BACKED SECURITIES

You can buy mortgage-backed securities through your bank or broker with roughly the same fee schedule as any other bonds. You would pay between 0.5 and 3 percent, depending on the size of the bond and some other factors.

Ginnie Mae securities come in denominations of $25,000 and higher. For those on a lower budget, you can buy Freddie Mac and Fannie Mae securities for $1000 or more. You can buy MBSs with 30-year terms or 15-year terms. In fact, by buying an MBS on the secondary market, you can pick one with nearly any duration you want.

As an MBS owner, you will receive payments every month representing both interest and a small portion of the principal.

Fannie Mae provides a help line for investors at 1-800-237-8627, or (202) 752-6547. The help line is staffed from 9 a.m. to 5:30 p.m., Eastern time, Monday through Friday.

BIGGEST CONCERNS

Mortgage-backed securities are very close to a worry-free investment. They pay relatively high rates and are considered very safe. They are readily available and are easy to buy and sell on the secondary market.

No question, the biggest concern for MBS owners is the prepayment risk and the extension risk. When rates are dropping, mortgage-backed securities typically get paid off early, so the investor's high rate of return is cut short early—during a period when it is more difficult to find high-yielding investments. During periods of low rates, you face an extension risk—the very high likelihood that if rates rise, homeowners will stick with their lower-interest mortgages through the full term, leaving you with a low return for years to come. Fortunately you do receive some compensation for that risk in the form of interest rates that average 1 to 2 percent higher than most government bonds.

TIMING

Timing is tough to judge with mortgage-backed securities because of the extension and prepayment risks. Do you buy when rates are high when you face the risk of having your mortgages paid off early if rates drop? Do you buy when rates are fairly low and face the risk of holding low-yielding securities later in a high-interest environment? There's no perfect answer.

The perfect pick for mortgage-backed securities would be to an MBS that represents a pool of older, lower-interest mortgages that the mortgage holders would be unlikely to pay off early. An MBS trades like any other bond—as interest rates rise, the price of older, lower-yielding mortgage-backed securities drops to compensate for the lower yields. So because of the discount, in times of rising interest rates you still get an MBS with a yield that is competitive with the rest of the fixed-income market. But because your MBS represents a pool of earlier mortgages with lower interest rates, your risk of prepayment is sharply reduced.

Otherwise, buying mortgage-backed securities is similar to buying other types of traditional bonds. During periods of low interest rates, you might want to buy a shorter-term MBS on the secondary market so that you are not stuck with a low yield for too long. During periods of high interest rates, you can buy an MBS and enjoy the high rates for as long as possible—particularly if you buy one that represents earlier, lower rates with a lower risk of prepayment. Either way, you're buying into an investment that should provide a better current yield than government bonds and many corporate bonds (which also carry a risk of early redemption).

In times of low interest, if you are choosing between Treasury issues (such as T-bonds and T-notes) and mortgage-backed securities, both could have very long terms, and mortgage securities pay a higher return, so that might be your best bet. During periods of high interest, you might want to invest a little more in Treasury issues because of their noncallable guarantee.

MONITORING YOUR MORTGAGE-BACKED SECURITIES

With billions of dollars in mortgage-backed securities on the market, there is no single source that provides price information on every issue.

However, you should receive periodic statements from the broker who sold you the MBS, giving the current status of the security, including the amount of principal that has been paid and the amount that remains to be paid.

You can find additional information on mortgage-backed securities at *www.investinginbonds.com*, *www.ginniemae.gov*, *www.fanniemae.com*, *www.hud.gov*, or *www.freddiemac.com*.

ASSET ALLOCATION

The amount of money you allocate toward mortgage-backed securities would depend on your tax situation, your financial situation, your investment goals, and your tolerance for risk.

Conservative investors concerned with preservation of capital might want to invest 20 to 60 percent of their assets in various fixed-income investments, including mortgage-backed securities, T-bonds, and corporate bonds under normal economic conditions. You might want to lighten the weighting of fixed-income securities in the portfolio during periods of low interest rates, and increase the weighting during periods of high interest.

Aggressive investors looking for long-term growth would probably want to limit their investment in MBSs, although they are more attractive than many other types of bonds because of their higher returns. An allocation of 5 to 20 percent of assets in fixed-income investments such as MBSs and government and corporate bonds, even for aggressive investors, would help provide balance and diversification for a portfolio that is heavily weighted in stocks.

SPECIAL CONSIDERATIONS

Mortgage-backed securities are commonly assessed based on "average life" rather than a stated maturity date. The average life is the average time that each principal dollar in the pool is expected to be outstanding, based upon preconceived assumptions about prepayment speeds. The average life is always a best estimate and could fluctuate based on how closely the prepayment speeds of the underlying mortgage loans compare with the initial assumptions.

12

ANNUITIES

Tax-Deferred Income and Capital Appreciation

ANNUITIES MIGHT BE KNOWN most for making big insurance companies even richer. Annuities generally come with some fairly hefty fees, but because of their very favorable tax benefits, annuities can still be a good deal for investors looking to park some retirement money.

An annuity is essentially a contract sold to an investor by an insurance company that pays a fixed or variable payment at some future period. Annuities are certainly not for everyone, but if you've put the maximum amount into your tax-deferred investment plan and you still have money that you want to put toward retirement, an annuity could be an enticing option.

Your money accumulates in an annuity tax-deferred, just as it does in an IRA or other retirement plan. However, there is no current-year income tax deduction for contributions to annuities as there is for IRAs and other government established retirement plans.

There are several variations of annuities—some come with immediate payouts, others with deferred payments; some pay a fixed return, others offer variable returns.

FIXED ANNUITIES

With a fixed annuity, an investor pays a sum of money to an insurance company and, in exchange, receives a guaranteed fixed monthly income for either a set period of time or for the rest of the investor's lifetime. Fixed annuities are available in several forms. If you have a lump sum to invest, you can fund your annuity with a single check, or you can pay into an annuity on a monthly or yearly basis for a period of years. With a lump-sum annuity, you can arrange to have the payments begin to you immediately, or you can have them deferred until later (after your retirement, for instance).

Fixed annuities tend to be very safe investments, but your return on investment is fairly low compared with other types of investment options.

VARIABLE ANNUITIES

A variable annuity gives investors more flexibility in their investment options. When you pay into a variable annuity, you can have the money invested in one of a variety of portfolios (similar to mutual funds), including stock portfolios or bond portfolios. You can also switch from portfolio to portfolio without additional fees and without paying taxes on your gains.

Unlike a fixed annuity, a variable annuity has no predetermined rate of return. The return is based on the performance of the portfolios you select. If you choose a stock portfolio that does well over the long-term, you would very likely receive a much better return than you would with a fixed annuity. On the other hand, if your portfolio does poorly, you could end up with a lower payout.

You can fund a variable annuity with one lump sum or a series of monthly payments. With a lump-sum annuity, you can have the payments deferred until later, or you can begin taking payments immediately. The amount of your payment in the years ahead would depend on the performance of your annuity portfolio.

Although variable annuities are considered to be riskier than fixed-income investments, in most cases, variable annuities pay a much higher return than fixed annuities.

WHO SHOULD BUY AN ANNUITY?

Annuities are geared to investors who want retirement income. An annuity might be right for you if you:

- Have already contributed the maximum to your IRA, 401k, or other tax-deferred retirement plan

- Plan to keep the annuity for at least 10 years

- Don't need the money until you're at least 59 $^{1}/_{2}$

- Are in a high tax bracket

- Want a guaranteed return—even if it's a lower return than you might get with other types of investments

WHO SHOULD *NOT* BUY AN ANNUITY?

You probably shouldn't buy an annuity if you:

- Have not contributed the maximum to your IRA or 401k retirement plan.

- Are not in a high tax bracket

- Might need the money before your retirement years

- Are an aggressive investor interested in getting the best possible return for your dollars.

RETURN

You don't buy an annuity because of the return. Annuities can provide some safety and the potential for capital appreciation, but there are other types of investments that might give you a higher return.

However, because of the tax-deferred status of an annuity, over the long term, your money might grow faster in an annuity than it would in mutual funds because annual mutual fund gains are taxable in the current year. Your investment in an annuity grows tax-free until you withdraw it, at which time it is taxed at your standard income tax rate.

Fixed annuities are considered very safe, with a guaranteed rate of return, however, that return tends to be relatively low compared with most other types of fixed-income investments.

Variable annuities typically pay higher returns than fixed annuities, but they carry more risk. For instance, if you have your money invested in a stock portfolio, when the market goes down that could cause your annual return to decline. But in a normal stock market, your returns would be better than the returns of a fixed annuity.

In a variable annuity that is invested in a stock portfolio, your returns would be similar to a stock mutual fund. However, annuities carry some extra charges that mutual funds don't. With an annuity, you would have to pay about 1 percent of assets per year over and above the typical mutual fund management fee.

However, that extra fee does provide a benefit—a *death* benefit—that mutual funds don't offer. With an annuity, if you die before you begin to receive income, your beneficiaries will receive at least the principal amount you put into your annuity. In fact, with most annuities, your investment gains are locked in regularly so that your beneficiaries receive more than your principal even if the value of the portfolio has declined by the time of your death. So that death benefit assures annuity buyers that they can't lose money even if they chose to have their money invested in stock portfolios. That's a huge benefit for conservative investors.

RISKS

The only risks you face with a fixed annuity is whether the company offering the annuity stays in business. And if you buy through a well-established insurance or investment company, there should be nothing to worry about. Your return is fixed at the time you buy the annuity.

There are greater risks with a variable annuity. Your return depends on the performance of the stock or bond portfolios to which you allocate your money. If the market is good, your returns will be solid. But even in a bad market, an annuity reduces your risks of loss (as explained in the above section).

UPSIDE

Annuities have several benefits, including:

- **Retirement income.** With either type of annuity, you can assure yourself of a steady stream of retirement income.

- **Tax-deferred growth.** Your annuity grows tax-deferred, which enables the money to accumulate in the account at a much faster pace.

- **Safety.** With a fixed-income annuity, you are assured of receiving exactly the monthly payment guaranteed in your contract. Even with variable annuities, in most cases you are assured that no matter how poorly the overall stock market performs, your principal will never fall below the amount you paid into the account.

- **Appreciation potential.** Variable annuities invested in stock portfolios can grow at a very nice pace if the overall market does well.

- **Tax-free, fee-free switching.** In a variable annuity, you have the option of switching from one type of portfolio to another (from a stock portfolio to a bond portfolio to a small stock portfolio, and so forth) without paying any additional fees or paying any taxes on your gains.

- **Flexibility.** You decide how much to contribute, when to contribute it, how to allocate the money, and when to begin taking payments.

DOWNSIDE

Annuities do have some notable drawbacks, including:

- **No liquidity.** If you buy an annuity, it should be for the long term. You could face some penalties and a loss of a good chunk of your investment if you try to withdraw your money early.

- **Lukewarm returns.** Fixed annuities offer fairly low returns as compared with other fixed-income investments, and variable annuities invested in stock portfolios tend to trail similar mutual funds in total return because of some additional fees charged to annuity holders.

- **Fully taxable upon withdrawal.** Unlike stocks and mutual funds, which are taxed a lower capital gains rate if you hold for the long term, annuity holders pay their full earned income rate when they begin withdrawing their profits from the fund.

- **Heirs are taxed on your gains.** When you die, your heirs will pay taxes on your gains at the ordinary income tax rate. With stocks, mutual funds, and other types of investments, they would qualify for a "step up" in the tax basis, which means they would pay no income taxes on the gains. However, because of the tax-deferred status of annuities, your assets could potentially grow at a much faster pace than they would in your personal mutual fund or stock account. So even after paying the income taxes, your heirs might still come out ahead with an annuity account.

HOW TO BUY ANNUITIES

You can buy an annuity through any life insurance agency as well as through many investment companies. Make a call to your insurance agent (or any insurance agency), and an agent will soon come calling on you to explain the company's annuity options in painful, droning detail.

But there is one more approach—use the Internet to comparison shop. There are several sites that allow you to compare annuity prices and options from several different companies. They even help you purchase an annuity online. Among the best sites for investors are *www.annuity.com*, *www.insure.com*, and *www.AnnuityScout.com*.

BIGGEST CONCERNS

Before you buy, do some comparison shopping to make sure you're getting the most for your money. There can be big differences in price and returns from one annuity company to another. Just don't spend too much.

If you buy a fixed annuity, you should also be sure to get enough coverage to have a decent stream of income throughout your retirement. If your retirement is many years away, try to figure in inflation. What might sound like a sufficient amount now might actually be a relatively small amount upon your retirement—and even smaller in future years. If you expect to need that money to live on during your retirement years, make sure you're not shortchanging yourself.

TIMING

There is no special time to buy an annuity, but if you own a variable annuity, you could try to time your movements within the annuity. When interest rates are high, you might want to move a good share of your assets into a bond portfolio. When interest rates are low, it might be time to move some of that money back into a stock portfolio. With an annuity, you can move your money freely from one portfolio to another without any fees or taxes.

MONITORING YOUR ANNUITIES

The only way to monitor your annuity is through the regular statements that the annuity company sends you in the mail. The statement should show the value of your annuity along with other pertinent details.

ASSET ALLOCATION

For those who choose to own an annuity, it should probably play a fairly minor role in your overall portfolio. First you should fund your IRA, 401k, or other retirement plan to the hilt before even considering buying an annuity. Life insurance should also take precedence over an annuity. Then make sure your shorter-term needs are met, such as money for down payment on a house, college savings for the kids, and any other expenses you will face prior to retirement. Once you've covered everything, and you still have some money left over that you won't need until you retire, that's when you buy an annuity. Even then, an annuity should be one small part of a much larger asset base that includes not only your retirement fund assets but also a diversified asset base of stocks, mutual funds, REITs, fixed-income investments, and other assets.

The higher your tax bracket and the greater your wealth, the more likely it would be that you could enjoy the benefits of an annuity.

SPECIAL CONSIDERATIONS

If you're buying a fixed annuity, you need to pay close attention to the financial strength of the annuity firm. With a fixed annuity, your premiums go into the company's general account. If the firm runs into some financial problems, your annuity principal could be in jeopardy. With variable annuities, unless you have a fixed account, your premiums go into a separate account that is insulated from the annuity company's own financials.

Before you buy a fixed annuity, you should check with a professional ratings service to determine the strength of the annuity company. You want a company with an A rating, if not higher (such as an AA, an AAA, an A+, or an A++). You can get ratings by phone for free from several services, including Standard & Poor's (212-438-2400), Fitch (800-853-4824), and Moody's (212-553-0377).

13

CORPORATE BONDS

Decent Income, Low Risk

C ORPORATE BONDS give you the chance to loan your hard-earned money to giant corporations such as 3M, GM, and GE. Companies use two means to raise money—they issue stock and they float bonds. When you buy stock, you're an owner of the company; when you buy bonds you are a lender to the company.

Corporate bonds of financially sound blue chip companies are considered very safe investments, and they pay slightly higher yields than government bonds. All bonds are rated by such investment services as Standard & Poor's or Moody's. Bonds rated BBB or higher (through AAA) by Standard & Poor's or Duff & Phelps, or Baa by Moody's are considered investment-grade bonds. Anything rated lower would be considered a "junk bond." (More on junk bonds in the next chapter.)

Most bonds pay interest semiannually. Depending on the financial creditworthiness of the issuing company, a corporate bond can yield from 1 to 3 percentage points more than Treasuries of the same maturity. (Junk bonds go even higher.)

Like all bonds, corporate bond prices are sensitive to general fluctuations in interest rates. They are also affected by the financial fortunes of the issuing companies. The price might rise if the company's finances improve because investors anticipate that the bond's safety rating might be upgraded. On the other hand, a company that experiences some financial problems could see its bond price decline because of investor fears that the rating will be downgraded.

Most corporate bonds are known as debentures because they are unsecured. The bonds are not backed by collateral, but simply by the company's general ability to repay them out of cash flow and profits.

Corporate bonds are also available in zero-coupon bonds. You would receive no payments until the bond matures, at which point you would receive the entire principal and all the interest compounded.

If you don't want to buy individual corporate bonds, there are dozens of mutual funds that specialize in corporate bonds.

WHO SHOULD BUY CORPORATE BONDS?

Investment-grade corporate bonds are appropriate for income-oriented and conservative investors who want a higher yield than would be available with government bonds. They also might be suitable for aggressive stock-oriented investors looking for diversification.

Aggressive investors looking for income might prefer corporate bonds over government bonds because of the superior interest rate, although there are a few other fixed-income investments that offer an even better return, such as junk bonds, REITs, and convertible bonds. (Convertibles don't offer quite the interest rate of corporate bonds, but they also provide some capital appreciation as part of the stock conversion value. See the chapter on "Convertible Securities.")

However, because corporate bonds pay fully taxable interest, unless you need the income, it would be best to use corporate bonds in your tax-deferred retirement account.

WHO SHOULD *NOT* BUY CORPORATE BONDS?

If you don't want income, corporate bonds are not for you (unless you buy a zero-coupon bond tied to a corporate bond).

If you want income but you want absolute safety, you might prefer government issues. But AAA-rated corporate bonds are considered very safe and offer better returns than government bonds.

Aggressive investors looking for the highest potential return might also steer away from corporate bonds. Although they pay a better yield than some fixed-income investments, they still fall short of junk bonds, REITs, and some other types of income-oriented investments, and they fall far short of the average annual return offered by stocks. However, corporate bonds are considered much safer than stocks for buy-and-hold investors.

RETURN

The return from corporate bonds is about 1 to 2 percent higher than Treasury issues with similar term lengths. Most bonds pay interest every six months.

Since 1925, investment-grade corporate bonds have provided an average annual return of about 5.8 percent. That is a better rate than money market funds, Treasury bills, and most short-term fixed-income investments, such as certificates of deposit. It is also a slightly better return than T-bonds, which have averaged 5.3 percent since 1925. High-yield (junk) bonds typically offer yields of 2 to 4 points higher than the AAA-rated corporate bonds. Blue chip stocks have been far better, on average, than corporate bonds, averaging 10.7 percent per year since 1925.

Figures 13-1 and 13-2 illustrate the comparison between corporate bonds and blue chip stocks.

RISKS

Investment-grade bonds, which are A-rated, are considered very safe, with very little chance of default. But they are a step down the safety ladder from government bonds, which are backed by the full faith and credit of the U.S. government.

If you hold a bond through to maturity, there is little risk of losing money. But you could take a loss on a corporate bond if you sell out early. Like all fixed-income investments, corporate bond prices go up as market interest rates go down, and prices go down as interest rates go up. So if you try to sell a bond in an environment of rising interest rates, you might have to take a loss on the sale.

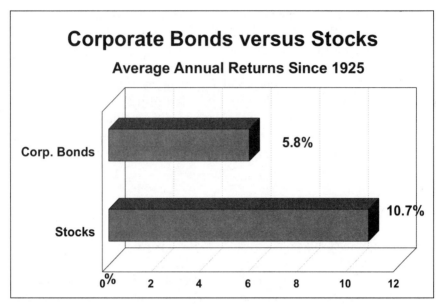

FIGURE 13-1

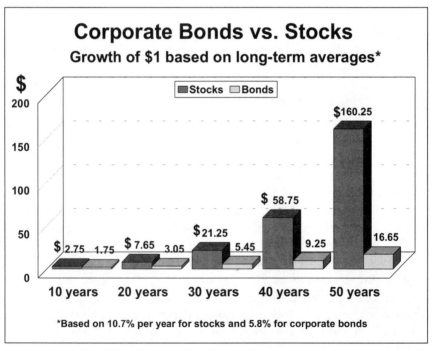

FIGURE 13-2

UPSIDE

Corporate bonds have several benefits, including:

- **Decent income.** They pay a higher rate than many government bonds, money markets, bank accounts, and certificates of deposit.

- **Liquidity.** There is a huge secondary market for most corporate bonds, so you can buy and sell them whenever you wish. If you don't want to hold them through maturity, it's easy to find a buyer on the secondary market.

- **Easy to buy.** They are easy to buy and can be purchased through your bank or your broker.

- **Safety.** Investment grade bonds (AAA-, AA-, and A-rated) are considered very safe investments, with little chance of default.

- **Appreciation potential.** Corporate bonds can increase in value if interest rates decline, so you could sell the bond at a profit on the secondary market.

DOWNSIDE

Corporate Bonds have some notable drawbacks, including:

- **Lukewarm returns.** Corporate bond returns might be better than most government issues, but they still fall behind many other income-based investments, such as REITs, junk bonds, mortgage-backed bonds, and others.

- **Callable.** If interest rates start falling, you might get your money back before you want it. Corporations typically redeem high-interest bonds early if interest rates decline.

- **Fully taxable.** Unlike government bonds, corporate bonds are fully taxable by federal, state, and local governments. Keep that in mind when comparing rates of corporate bonds with government bonds (exempt from state and local taxes) and municipal bonds (exempt from federal taxes and sometimes state and local taxes).

- **Potential for loss.** If you hold a bond through to maturity, you'll get your principal back in full, but the value of your bond on the secondary market could drop if market interest rates rise.

HOW TO BUY CORPORATE BONDS

You can buy corporate bonds through your bank or broker with roughly the same fee schedule as any other bonds. You would pay between 0.5 and 3 percent, depending on the size of the order, the availability of the bonds, and some other factors. In dollar terms, you could pay a per-bond commission of $2.50 to $30. ($30 would be 3 percent on a $1000 bond).

Corporate bonds come with par values of $1000, although brokers like to trade in blocks of 5 to 10 bonds. There are some "baby bonds" with smaller par values of $250 or $500.

Corporate bonds come with maturities ranging from very short (two or three years) to very long (as much as 30 years). Typically, the longer the term of the bond the higher the yield.

BIGGEST CONCERNS

The two biggest concerns with investment-grade corporate bonds are the investment risk and the possibility of early redemption.

If you plan to hold a bond to maturity, there is no investment risk. But if you buy a bond with a low interest rate, and market rates start to climb, the value of your bond on the secondary market would decline, so you could lose money if you sell the bond early.

On the other hand, if you buy a bond with a high interest rate, and market rates begin to decline, the value of your bond should increase. But then you face the second threat—the possibility of recall. When interest rates drop, corporations often pay off their higher interest bonds and issue new bonds at lower rates. If your bond is recalled, you receive your principal back in full, but those high-interest-rate payments will come to a stop, and you would have to buy new bonds at a lower rate of interest.

Before buying a long-term bond, find out what kind of call protection the bond has. Some issuers guarantee that they will not recall their bonds for a set number of years. Others offer no call protection. That might not be an issue when interest rates are rising, but if they are high and starting to fall, call protection becomes a very important issue.

TIMING

The best time to buy a corporate bond—or nearly any fixed-rate investment—is when interest rates are high. The worst time is when interest rates are low. During periods of low interest rates, you might want to buy a shorter-term bond on the secondary market so you are not stuck with a low yield for too long. During periods of high interest rates, you can buy a longer-term bond and enjoy the high rates for as long as possible—particularly if you buy one that represents earlier, lower rates with a lower risk of prepayment.

If you want to buy a bond during a period of falling interest rates, but you want to avoid having your high-interest-rate bond recalled early, you should try to buy an older bond on the secondary market that has a lower coupon rate than current bonds. When low-yield bonds trade on the secondary market, they sell at a discount, which brings their current yield up to the same level as market interest rates. So you get essentially the same yield as other bonds, but you would probably avoid the threat of early recall because corporations are not likely to recall bonds that have interest rates lower than current market rates.

MONITORING YOUR CORPORATE BONDS

You can find price and yield information on most bonds in the leading financial publications. But there is an even better source online—a free Web site operated by the NASD, Inc. (National Association of Securities Dealers) at *www.nasdbondinfo.com*. The site provides current prices and yields for hundreds of bonds.

You can find additional information on corporate bonds at *www.investinginbonds.com* and *www.bondsonline.com.*

ASSET ALLOCATION

The amount of money you allocate toward corporate bonds would depend on your tax situation, your financial situation, your investment goals, and your threshold for risk.

Conservative investors concerned with preservation of capital might want to invest 20 to 60 percent of their assets in various fixed-income investments such as corporate bonds, mortgage-backed securities, T-bonds, and convertibles. You might want to lighten the weighting of fixed-income securities in the portfolio during periods of low interest rates, and increase the weighting during periods of high interest.

Aggressive investors looking for long-term growth would probably want to limit their investment in corporate bonds, although they are more attractive than many other types of bonds because of their higher returns. An allocation of 5 to 20 percent of assets in fixed-income investments such as corporate bonds, mortgage-backed securities, or zero-coupon bonds, even for aggressive investors, would help provide balance and diversification for a portfolio that is heavily weighted in stocks.

SPECIAL CONSIDERATIONS

When shopping for bonds, many investors look at the *current yield,* which is the annual return based on the dollar amount paid for a bond. So if you paid $100 for a bond and it pays $10 a year in interest, the bond would have a current yield of 10 percent.

But a better measure to judge the market value of a bond—particularly on the secondary market—is *yield to maturity*. It tells you the total return you will receive if you hold a bond until maturity—including all interest and capital gains (if you buy the bond on the secondary market at a discount) or capital loss (if you buy the bond at a premium). That's a good way to compare bonds with different maturities and coupon interest rates.

However, there is one more factor to consider when comparing the bond yields—the recall factor. If you buy a bond with a great yield to maturity, but the company recalls the bond the next year, that could turn out to be a bad investment. Look at current yield, look at yield to maturity, but look very closely at each bond's call protection and the possibility that the company might recall the bond early. Try to find bonds with good call protection and a good yield to maturity.

14

JUNK BONDS

High Income with Risk

IF YOU WANT HIGH RISK with high reward, junk bonds might be the investment for you. Also known as "high-yield bonds," junk bonds are corporate bonds issued by companies that are on less stable financial footing. That might include newer, smaller companies that need to raise capital to expand their businesses or established companies facing financial difficulty. Junk bonds pay a much higher yield than investment-grade corporate bonds and Treasury issues.

As an investor, if you have a choice between investing in a bond from a big blue chip company such as Johnson & Johnson or Procter & Gamble or one from a company you've never heard of, you would probably prefer the one from the blue chip firm. That's why riskier companies must pay higher yields than blue chip companies. If the choice is between a General Motors bond paying 5 percent or an XYZ Corp. bond paying 10 percent, suddenly the junk bond starts to look a lot more enticing.

In reality, very few junk bonds ever default, but the threat is always there, which means that a certain amount of risk goes with the territory. There is also the risk that the company's bonds could be downgraded further, reducing the value of the bonds and making them more difficult to sell on the secondary market. But if the company survives, your returns would be outstanding.

Bonds rated BBB or higher by Standard & Poor's or Duff & Phelps, or Baa by Moody's are considered investment-grade bonds. Anything rated lower would be considered a junk bond.

There is one option that allows you to reduce your risk while still collecting the high returns that junk bonds offer—a junk bond mutual fund. There are dozens of mutual funds that specialize in junk bonds, and they have become very popular with individual investors.

WHO SHOULD BUY JUNK BONDS?

Junk bonds are appropriate for aggressive income-oriented investors interested in a high rate of return as part of a diversified portfolio.

However, because junk bonds pay fully taxable interest, unless you need the income, it would be best to use junk bonds in your tax-deferred retirement account.

WHO SHOULD *NOT* BUY JUNK BONDS?

If you don't want income, junk bonds are not for you.

If you *do* want income, but you want it with a minimum of risk, junk bonds would not be an appropriate investment. However, a junk bond mutual fund would be a much safer investment, while still providing a very high rate of return. Even for conservative investors, a junk bond fund would be a suitable investment as a *small* part of a diversified portfolio. But if you don't need income, you might want to use a junk bond fund in your tax-deferred retirement account.

RETURN

The return from junk bonds can be 3 to 7 percent higher than Treasury issues with similar term lengths, and 2 to 6 percent higher than investment-grade corporate bonds. The riskier the bond, the higher the yield.

All bonds are rated by services such as Moody's Investor Service, Standard & Poor's, or Duff & Phelps. The rate of interest they pay is based on their risk rating. The lower the bond rating, the higher the interest they have to pay to attract investors. So different junk bonds have different rates of return. The return of the higher-yielding junk bonds approaches the average annual return of the stock market (10.7 percent since 1925). Over the past 20 years, yields offered by junk bonds have ranged from about 7 percent in recent years to as high as 20 percent during the early 1980s.

Most corporate bonds, including junk bonds, pay interest twice a year.

RISKS

Despite the name, junk bonds are not as risky as you might think. Very, very few junk bonds ever default, but it can happen to a small company in a down economy. That's why a junk bond mutual fund that owns a wide range of different bonds would be a safer, easier investment for individual investors.

If you hold a bond through to maturity, there is little risk of losing money aside from the risk of default. But you could take a loss on a junk bond if you sell out early. Like all fixed-income investments, junk bond prices go up as market interest rates go down, and prices go down as interest rates go up. So if you try to sell a bond in an environment of rising interest rates, you might have to take a loss on the sale.

UPSIDE

Junk bonds have several important benefits that keep aggressive investors coming back, such as:

- **Good income.** They pay a higher rate than any other type of bond.

- **Liquidity.** There is a huge secondary market for most junk bonds, so you can buy and sell them whenever you wish. If you don't want to hold them through maturity, it's easy to find a buyer on the secondary market.

- **Easy to buy.** They are easy to buy and can be purchased through your bank or your broker.

- **Appreciation potential.** Junk bonds can increase in value if interest rates decline, so you could sell the bond at a profit on the secondary market.

DOWNSIDE

While they pay a very attractive rate of return, junk bonds do have some notable drawbacks, including:

- **Risk.** The biggest downside to junk bonds is the risk. They have a higher risk of default than any other type of bond—but then, that's why they pay the high yields.

- **Callable.** If interest rates start falling, you might get your money back before you want it. Corporations typically redeem high-interest bonds early if interest rates decline.

- **Fully taxable**. Unlike government bonds, junk bonds are fully taxable by federal, state, and local governments. But, despite the extra taxes you would pay on junk bonds, the comparable after-tax return is still much higher with junk bonds than it would be with any type of government or municipal bond.

- **Potential for loss**. If you hold a bond through to maturity, you'll get your principal back in full, but the value of your bond on the secondary market could drop if market interest rates rise. So if you try to sell it before maturity, you might have to settle for a loss on your original principal.

HOW TO BUY JUNK BONDS

You can buy junk bonds through your bank or broker with roughly the same fee schedule as any other bonds. You would pay between 0.5 and 3 percent, depending on the size of the order, the availability of the bonds, and some other factors. In dollar terms, you could pay a per-bond commission of $2.50 to $30. ($30 would be 3 percent on a $1000 bond).

Junk bonds come with par values of $1000, although brokers like to trade in blocks of 5 to 10 bonds. There are some "baby bonds" with smaller par values of $250 or $500.

Junk bonds come with maturities ranging from very short (2 or 3 years) to very long (as much as 30 years). Typically, the longer the term of the bond, the higher the yield.

BIGGEST CONCERNS

The two biggest concerns with junk bonds are the investment risk and the possibility of early redemption.

If you plan to hold a bond to maturity, there is no investment risk. But if you buy a bond with a low interest rate, and market rates start to climb, the value of your bond on the secondary market would decline, so you could lose money if you sell the bond early.

On the other hand, if you buy a bond with a high interest rate, and market rates begin to decline, the value of your bond should increase. But then you face the second threat—the possibility of recall. When interest rates drop, corporations often pay off their higher-interest bonds and issue new bonds at lower rates. If your bond is recalled, you receive your principal back in full, but those high-interest-rate payments will come to a stop, and you would have to buy new bonds at a lower rate of interest.

Before buying a long-term junk bond, find out what kind of call protection the bond has. Some issuers guarantee that they will not recall their bonds for a set number of years. Others offer no call protection. That might not be an issue when interest rates are rising, but if they are high and starting to fall, call protection becomes a very important factor.

TIMING

The best time to buy a junk bond—or nearly any fixed-rate investment—is when interest rates are high. The worst time is when interest rates are low. During periods of low interest rates, you might want to buy a shorter-term bond on the secondary market so that you are not stuck with a low yield for too long. During periods of high interest rates, you can buy a longer-term bond and enjoy the high rates for as long as possible—particularly if you buy one that represents earlier, lower rates with a lower risk of prepayment.

If you want to buy a bond during a period of falling interest rates, but you want to avoid having your high-interest-rate bond recalled early, you should try to buy an older bond on the secondary market that has a lower coupon rate than current bonds. When low-yield bonds trade on the secondary market, they sell at a discount, which brings their current yield up to the same level as market interest rates. So you get essentially the same yield as other bonds, but you would probably avoid the threat of early recall because corporations are not likely to recall bonds that have interest rates lower than current market rates.

MONITORING YOUR JUNK BONDS

Your broker might be the best source of information on junk bonds, but you can find price and yield information on many junk bonds in the leading financial publications. You can also find information on some junk bonds online at a free Web site operated by the NASD, Inc. (National Association of Securities Dealers) at *www.nasdbondinfo.com*. The site provides current prices and yields for hundreds of bonds.

You can find additional information on junk bonds at *www.investing-inbonds.com* and *www.bondsonline.com.*

ASSET ALLOCATION

The amount of money you allocate toward junk bonds would depend on your tax situation, your financial situation, your investment goals, and your threshold for risk.

Conservative investors concerned with preservation of capital might not want any exposure to junk bonds. But holding a junk bond as part of a diversified bond portfolio would provide a little better return while keeping your risk of loss to a minimum.

Income-oriented investors looking for the best possible return might consider owning several different junk bonds along with some other safer fixed-income investments in order to minimize the risk. A better idea might be to buy junk bond mutual funds.

Aggressive investors looking for long-term growth might like some junk bonds or junk bond funds in the portfolio. An allocation of 5 to 20 percent of assets in fixed-income investments such as junk bonds, corporate bonds, mortgage-backed securities, or zero-coupon bonds, even for aggressive investors, would help provide balance and diversification for a portfolio that is heavily weighted in stocks.

SPECIAL CONSIDERATIONS

There is a fine line in choosing a junk bond between rate of return and level of risk. The higher the return, the more you'll make, but the bigger the chance of default. Before buying a junk bond, check out the financial strength of the underlying company (or have your broker check it out). You might find that it's worthwhile to sacrifice a percentage point or two in returns in exchange for a little more safety.

CONVERTIBLE SECURITIES

Income and Capital Appreciation

PART STOCK, PART BOND, convertible securities give you a taste of both worlds, with the opportunity to earn interest and capital appreciation.

Convertibles come in two forms: *convertible preferred stock* (not to be confused with the more common nonconvertible preferred stock that trades on the major stock exchanges) and *debentures*, which are unsecured bonds. Both pay a fixed rate of interest and are convertible into common stock of the issuer when the common stock reaches a certain price, known as the conversion price. When the convertible is issued, the conversion price is set at a level 15 to 50 percent higher than the common stock's price. When the stock hits the conversion price, the convertible can be exchanged for a preset number of shares at the "conversion ratio." For example, a convertible bond for XYZ Corp. might have a conversion price of $50 a share and a conversion ratio of 30-to-1. That means bondholders would be allowed to convert each bond into 30 shares of XYZ stock when the stock hits $50 a share.

Convertible bonds are considered safer and less volatile than stocks, but they don't have the long-term average annual return of stocks, nor do they pay quite as high an interest rate as normal corporate bonds. But bonds don't have the capital appreciation potential that convertibles do. As the price of the underlying stock rises, the convertible price rises as well—just not as quickly as the stock price.

Convertibles are affected by a couple of important forces—*investment value* and *conversion value*. Like bonds, they are sensitive to interest rate fluctuations. If market interest rates rise, that can lower the *investment value* of a convertible. But interest rate swings don't affect convertibles quite as much as they do bonds because the convertible's price is also tied to the stock price. If the stock price is moving up to a level close to the conversion price, interest rate fluctuations wouldn't have much effect on the price of the convertible. Its price would be more closely tied to the stock because of its *conversion value*. On the other hand, if the stock is not doing well, but interest rates are holding steady, the price of the convertible would be buoyed by its yield and would trade more like a bond.

Convertibles are callable by the company, so if the company can cash them out during times of declining interest and issue new bonds with lower yields, they often will. Otherwise, investors are expected to cash out the bonds about when the stock hits the conversion price. Or when the stock's dividend becomes as high or higher than the convertible's yield, that's a sure sign that it's time to convert into common shares.

To some investors, convertibles offer the best of both worlds—relatively high fixed income and solid appreciation potential. But to others, they represent the worst of both worlds—lower yields than many bonds and less appreciation potential than common stocks. But they do offer a better long-term return than most other investments on the market, and they can help bring balance and diversification to a portfolio without sacrificing too much in performance.

WHO SHOULD BUY CONVERTIBLES?

Convertibles might appeal to investors interested in income, capital appreciation, and a fair level of safety. Conservative investors might like the fact that convertibles are somewhat less volatile than common stocks, while aggressive investors might like the fact that they offer higher potential for total return than bonds. Convertibles can provide diversification for an investment portfolio without significantly diminishing the total return potential.

WHO SHOULD *NOT* BUY CONVERTIBLE BONDS?

If you don't want income, you might not want to add convertibles to the portfolio.

Aggressive investors seeking the highest total return rarely buy convertibles because they tend to underperform stocks over the long-term. But in terms of adding diversification to the portfolio, it's hard to find an income-oriented investment with better return potential than convertibles.

Income-oriented investors might be able to get higher interest rates with standard corporate bonds and other types of fixed-income investments, but convertibles provide better total return potential than most bonds because of their conversion feature.

RETURN

Generally speaking, the total return offered by convertibles tends to be better than corporate bonds (which have averaged 5.8 percent since 1925) but worse than stocks (which have averaged 10.7 percent). The interest rate paid by convertibles tends to trail the corporate bond market slightly. So if IBM has a corporate bond that pays 6 percent, its convertible bonds might pay 5 percent. But the conversion feature of convertible bonds gives them a capital appreciation potential that bonds don't have. Convertibles can appreciate in value if the company's common stock is moving up, and convertible owners can cash in their bonds for stocks at a nice profit when the stock hits the conversion price.

RISKS

The risks are fairly low for convertible bonds of blue chip companies. In order to lose a large share of your investment on a convertible bond, the underlying company would have to go through a serious downturn.

Because of their investment value and their conversion value, convertible bonds tend to be more stable than either stocks or bonds. While they are sensitive to interest rate fluctuations, they are not as sensitive as bonds because their price is also tied to the price of the stock. And while they are sensitive to moves in the stock market—they rise and fall in moderation as the underlying stock fluctuates—they are not as volatile as stocks because of the investment value of their interest-bearing component.

UPSIDE

Convertibles offer several excellent benefits, including:

- **Interest income.** They pay regular interest income, which tends to be higher than many types of fixed-income investments, such CDs, savings bonds, T-bills and T-notes, but lower than corporate bonds and about the same as T-bonds.

- **Capital appreciation.** Because of their conversion feature, convertible bonds generally appreciate in value and are ultimately cashed in for stocks—at a profit—when the stock price hits a specific target price.

- **Liquidity.** There is a huge, well-organized market for convertibles, so they are easy to unload whenever you wish.

- **Easy to buy.** Convertibles can be purchased through any broker.

- **Easy to follow.** Convertible prices and interest rates are listed in the leading financial publications and online.

- **Safety.** Although they come with no guarantees, convertibles of blue chip companies are relatively safe because of their investment value and their conversion value. However, if a company's stock collapses, convertible bondholders can lose money. But convertibles are far less volatile than stocks. One other benefit is that convertibles are legal debt securities, so in case the company defaults, convertible owners take precedence over stock owners in collecting debt.

DOWNSIDE

Convertibles have few drawbacks, but they do have their detractors. Here are some of the key drawbacks of convertible bonds:

- **Callable.** Convertibles are callable. That means if you buy a convertible bond with a high interest rate, if rates start to drop, the company might pay off your bond early in order to issue new bonds at a lower interest rate. Frequently with convertibles, the company forces the bondholders to convert to stocks in what is known as a "forced conversion."

- **Taxable**. Unless you put your convertibles into a tax-deferred retirement plan, you will owe state, local, and federal income taxes on all interest payments. And if you sell the convertible or the stocks you get by converting your bond, you would owe capital gains taxes on your profits. However, if you hold onto the stocks, you will owe no taxes on your gains until you sell the stocks.

- **Lower interest rates than bonds**. If you're interested strictly in income, there are other investments that might give you better returns, such as corporate bonds, mortgage-backed securities, and REITs.

- **Lower appreciation potential than stocks**. If you're interested strictly in capital appreciation, stocks tend to outperform convertibles over the long-term.

HOW TO BUY CONVERTIBLES

You can't buy convertible securities through most online brokerages. You would probably require the services of a full-service broker. Convertibles usually come in minimum denominations of $1000, although most brokers prefer to trade in larger blocks of 10 to 25 bonds at a time. There are exceptions for investors interested in smaller lots called "baby bonds" that sell for as little as $50 to $500.

To buy convertible bonds, you would pay the broker a commission in the range of $5 to $30, depending on the broker and the size of the trade. A very large order would require a higher commission (but at a lower percentage). If you order one bond or a small lot, you would probably face a higher percentage markup by your broker.

Instead of owning individual convertibles, small investors might be interested in buying one of several mutual funds that focus on convertible securities.

BIGGEST CONCERNS

The two biggest concerns with convertibles are the underlying strength of the issuing company and the call protection of the bonds. Find out how much call protection the convertible offers. Don't buy a bond unless it has a reasonable period of call protection. Otherwise, the company could redeem the bond if interest rates fall and issue new bonds at lower rates.

Before you buy, you also need to check out the financial strength of the issuing company. If the company is solid, with AAA ratings for its corporate bonds and a history of consistent performance in the stock market, its convertible should be a sound investment.

TIMING

As with stocks, you want to buy convertibles when the price is low and sell (if you are so inclined) if the price is high. Convertibles can be a good investment during periods of low interest rates when you would rather not tie up your money with long-term bonds that could fall in value if interest rates were to move back up. Although convertibles are somewhat sensitive to interest rates—like other bonds—they are affected less because of their conversion value. So while other fixed-income investments might be dropping in value during a period of rising interest rates, convertibles might be holding steady or even increasing in value if the price of the stock is climbing.

The best time to own convertibles is when interest rates are high and stocks are climbing. That gives you a double boost—strong income and appreciation.

MONITORING YOUR CONVERTIBLES

Finding information on convertible debentures is not so easy. Your broker would be your best source of information on your convertible's price and current yield.

You can, however, find price and yield information on most bonds at a free Web site operated by the NASD, Inc. at *www.nasdbondinfo.com.*

Another resource is the ValueLine Convertibles Survey, although it's a little pricey. The cost is $525 a year or $65 for a three-month trial subscription. It ranks more than 600 convertibles for potential risk and return. You can sign up online at *www.valueline.com* or call 800-535-8760 to order or send a check to ValueLine Convertible Survey, 220 E. 42nd St., New York, NY 10017. The newsletter is mailed out weekly, and it is also available online.

ASSET ALLOCATION

The amount of money you allocate toward convertibles would depend on your tax situation, your financial situation, your investment goals, and your threshold for risk.

If you're a conservative investor concerned with preservation of capital, you might want to include convertibles as part of your fixed-income holdings. Conservative investors might want to keep 20 to 60 percent of their assets in various bonds and convertible securities.

Aggressive investors looking for long-term growth would probably want to limit their investment in convertibles, although convertibles are one of the best investments on the market for long-term growth. Convertibles can also provide diversification for an aggressive portfolio—and help lower the volatility—without significantly diminishing the long-term return potential of a portfolio that is made up primarily of stocks.

SPECIAL CONSIDERATIONS

Before you buy a convertible, make sure the company is on sound financial footing. A high interest rate can be enticing, but if the company is in financial trouble, that high interest rate might be fool's gold. You don't want to own a convertible for a company at risk of default because it can dramatically affect the price of the bond.

16

BOND MUTUAL FUNDS

Income and Diversification

U NLESS YOU HAVE SOME BIG BUCKS to throw at the market, building a diversified portfolio of bonds could be financially prohibi-
tive. But a bond mutual fund gives a smaller investor an
opportunity to become a shareholder in a diversified portfolio of bonds. You
can invest in bond funds with as little as $500 to $1000 and get instant diversification and professional management.

Bond funds hold dozens of different bonds with different maturity dates,
providing instant diversification for fund shareholders. Bond funds first
became popular in the 1970s, when investors began opting for managed
portfolios of bonds rather than individual bonds.

An offshoot of the traditional bond fund is the *high-yield bond funds* or
"junk bond funds." Safety is a major concern with individual junk bonds,
so the diversification that a mutual fund offers makes it a much safer investment. Even if one or two of the bonds in the fund default, the ultimate
impact on shareholders is minimal. But if you own an individual bond that
defaults, that can be a major shock to your bottom line.

Over the years, the universe of bond funds has exploded. Now they
come in many different forms, including:

- Corporate bond funds
- Junk bond funds
- Municipal (tax-exempt) bond funds
- Government bond funds
- Mortgage-backed bond funds
- Global bond funds
- Broad bond funds that invest in several types of bonds
- Money market funds

Whatever the type of bond that interests you, there's probably a bond fund that specializes in it.

WHO SHOULD BUY BOND FUNDS?

Bond funds are appropriate for income-oriented and conservative investors who want to earn a steady income with a minimum of risk. They might also be suitable for aggressive stock-oriented investors looking for diversification.

Aggressive investors looking for income might prefer high-yield bond funds or global bond funds over other types of bond funds because of the better returns. Conservative investors might want a combination of corporate, government, global, mortgage-backed, and high-yield funds. Affluent investors looking for additional income might prefer municipal bond funds because of the tax savings.

However, unless you need the income, you should use bond funds primarily for your tax-deferred retirement fund, with one exception—tax-exempt municipal bond funds. There's no point in putting a tax-exempt fund into a tax-deferred account.

WHO SHOULD *NOT* BUY BOND FUNDS?

If you don't want income, bond funds are probably not for you.

If you want income but you want absolute safety, individual government bonds are safer than bond funds. Government bonds have essentially no risk of default and no investment risk if you hold through maturity. But bond mutual funds all have investment risk because rising interest rates can cause the bonds in the fund's portfolio to drop in value—even government bonds.

Aggressive investors looking for the highest potential return should steer away from most bond funds, although junk bond funds, mortgage-backed bond funds, and some global bond funds would be a good choice. Those types of higher-yielding funds add diversification while providing a very respectable return on investment. But because of the tax implications, unless you need the income, it would be better to buy bond funds (except municipal bond funds) for your tax-sheltered retirement account.

Money market funds are not suitable long-term investments for any type of investor because their yield tends to be lower than most other bonds, but they are a safe place to stash money for the short term.

RETURN

The comparative yield from bond funds is almost a mirror image of the bonds themselves. Junk bond funds typically pay the highest returns, followed by global bond funds or mortgage-backed bond funds, corporate bond funds, government bond funds, tax-exempt municipal bond funds, and money market funds.

Bond fund returns are not quite the same as bonds themselves because the value of the bond fund portfolio continues to fluctuate. There is no maturity date with a bond fund as there is with a bond, so your principal investment is never assured. It could rise or fall depending on the direction of interest rates.

Mutual fund yields are similar to individual bond returns, but with some extra expenses to compensate the mutual fund managers. The best value is a no-load bond fund. No-load funds charge no fee to buy shares of the fund. But even the no-load funds charge annual management fees of about 1 to 2 percent, and that can have a dramatic impact on the fund's annual yield.

But it could be worse. If you use a broker to buy a fund, he or she will probably sell you a load fund. Load funds charge about 4 to 8 percent just to buy the fund—which is as much or more than the entire annual yield paid by many bond funds. In other words, your entire first-year earnings would be wiped out by the front-end load. On top of that, load funds (like no-loads) also charge annual management fees of about 1 to 2 percent.

RISKS

Bond mutual funds reduce the risk of owning some types of bonds and actually increase the risk of owning others.

With corporate and junk bonds and global bonds, a fund reduces the risk because it holds a broad portfolio of bonds. If one bond defaults, that would have little effect on the total return of the portfolio. By contrast, if you owned an individual bond that defaulted, that could have a major impact on your personal investment portfolio.

Government bonds and mortgage-backed securities are already almost as safe as cash itself, so pooling those types of bonds into a mutual fund would not add to investor safety. If you buy a safe government bond and hold it through to maturity, there would be no risk of losing money on your initial investment.

However, fluctuations in interest rates affect the market price of the bonds within a fund. In a rising interest environment, you can actually lose money in a government bond fund (or any bond fund). When interest rates rise, bond values drop. A 2-percent rise in market interest rates can push the value of a bond fund down by 10 percent or more. (Conversely, when market rates fall, bond fund prices appreciate.) That's why government bond funds are actually riskier than the bonds themselves.

UPSIDE

Bond funds have many benefits, including:

- **Diversification.** Bond funds have a broad portfolio of bonds, providing excellent diversification and lowering the risk of loss due to default.

- **Professional management**. Professional investment managers do the work for you.

- **Income.** Bond funds pay a yield similar to the type of bonds they hold, ranging from low-yielding government bond funds to high-yielding junk bond funds.

- **Liquidity.** With most funds, you can pull your money out simply by calling the company and telling them to sell your shares.

- **Low investment requirements.** It doesn't take a lot of money to invest in a mutual fund. Initial minimum investment requirements vary from about $250 to $2500 for most funds. And once you're a shareholder, most funds allow you to contribute even smaller subsequent amounts—usually in the range of $50 to $250—so it becomes very easy even for small investors to build a position in a fund.

- **Direct purchases.** Although brokers are often helpful in recommending good mutual funds to their clients, you don't have to use a broker to buy shares in a mutual fund. You can buy shares directly from the company simply by calling the company's toll-free sales line.

- **Checking deduction plans.** With most funds, you can have money automatically withdrawn from your checking account and invested in the fund each month or each quarter.

- **Automatic reinvestment.** With most mutual funds, investors can have their dividends and capital gains distributions automatically reinvested in additional shares of the fund with no additional sales fee.

- **Automatic withdrawal.** Retired investors sometimes opt for withdrawal plans that authorize the fund to pay out a set amount to the investor from his or her fund account each month or each quarter.

- **Appreciation potential**. Bond funds can increase in value if interest rates decline.

DOWNSIDE

Bond funds have a couple of notable drawbacks, including:

- **Fees.** Annual fees and loads (for the load funds) can cut into your total return.

- **Potential for loss**. Bond funds can decline in value if interest rates rise.

HOW TO BUY BOND FUNDS

You can buy load bond funds through your bank or broker, but if you want a no-load fund, the best way to buy it is through the mutual fund company. You can also buy no-loads through brokers, but you might face an extra fee to compensate the broker. (For more on charges, see "Return" on the previous page.)

All mutual fund companies have toll-free numbers that you can call to set up an account and get additional information on their funds.

You can find information on mutual fund performance in a number of publications. *Money* magazine, *Baron's*, *Consumer Reports*, and several other publications offer rankings of hundreds of funds in periodic special editions. Many investment Web sites also have fund rankings. You can use those rankings to find funds that have had solid returns for many years. Try to find a fund (or funds) that has been among the leaders in total return for the most recent five-year period—and have had good returns on a yearly basis for at least the past five years.

BIGGEST CONCERNS

Before you buy a bond fund, you should check on a few things. How has the fund performed in the past few years? You want one that has been among the leaders in total return and consistency.

Once you find a fund with a good track record, make sure the fund manager who established that track record is still with the fund.

Finally, check on fees. If possible, buy a no-load fund instead of a load fund—that will save you a lot of money up front. Then compare annual management fees. There can be a big difference from one fund to another. You might find fees as low as 1 percent or as high as 2.5 percent. With a portfolio of bonds that are paying only 4 or 5 percent, that extra 1.5 percent per year in fees could make a significant difference in your return.

TIMING

As with all fixed-income investments, the best time to buy a bond mutual fund is when interest rates are high because you get a good return and, if rates start to drop, the value of your fund shares would go up.

The worst time to buy would be when interest rates are low. Not only would you get a low return on investment, you could also see the value of your shares decline if market interest rates start to climb.

MONITORING YOUR BOND FUNDS

You can find information on mutual funds, including price and yield, in business newspapers and all over the Web. *The Wall Street Journal* has a huge special section on thousands of mutual funds every three months. On the Web, *Morningstar.com* and *multexinvestor.com* are two of the best sites for mutual fund information. America Online and Yahoo also have a wealth of current information on thousands of funds, as do dozens of other financial Web sites, such as *www.allstarStocks.com* and *www.money.cnn.com*.

ASSET ALLOCATION

The amount of money you allocate toward bond mutual funds would depend on your tax situation, your financial situation, your investment goals and your threshold for risk.

Conservative investors concerned with preservation of capital might want to invest 20 to 60 percent of their assets in various fixed-income investments such as bond funds, corporate bonds, mortgage-backed securities, T-bonds, and convertibles. You might want to lighten the weighting of bond funds and fixed-income securities in the portfolio during periods of low interest rates, and increase the weighting during periods of high interest.

Aggressive investors looking for long-term growth would probably want to limit their investment in the lower-yielding bond funds, but might opt for some shares of a junk bond fund, a mortgage-backed bond fund, or a global bond fund, which offer higher yields. An allocation of 5 to 20 percent of assets in bond funds or other fixed-income investments, even for aggressive investors, would help provide balance and diversification for a portfolio that is heavily weighted in stocks.

SPECIAL CONSIDERATIONS

There are some funds that mix stocks with bonds (usually referred to as balanced funds). If you want some exposure to bonds, but don't want to buy a bond fund, a balanced fund might be right for you. They usually have an asset mix somewhere in the range of 20 to 40 percent bonds and 60 to 80 percent stocks, although the mix can change as economic factors dictate.

17

STOCK MUTUAL FUNDS

Capital Appreciation, Income, and Diversification

Q UICK, CONVENIENT, AND DIVERSIFIED, mutual funds can be an excellent way to participate in the stock market. No poring over stock tables, no thumbing through annual reports and corporate balance sheets, no restless nights fretting over which stocks to buy and which to sell. All of that is done for you when you own a stock mutual fund.

Stock funds hold dozens, if not hundreds, of different stocks, and they are managed by investment professionals who do all of the buying and selling of stocks within the fund. When you own shares of a mutual fund, you become a part owner of that entire portfolio of stocks.

Stock funds come in many forms. In fact, the biggest problem for fund investors might be finding the right fund (or funds) out of the thousands of stock funds currently on the market. In all, there are about 8000 different mutual funds on the U.S. market.

There are funds to meet the tastes and risk thresholds of nearly everyone who invests. The original mutual funds were designed to produce a combination of growth and income by investing in a diversified portfolio of dividend-paying blue-chip stocks. Many such "growth and income" funds are still offered today—along with a host of other types of funds, including:

- **Long-term growth funds.** These funds invest primarily in stocks of growing blue chip companies in order to provide long-term appreciation (with minimal current income) for shareholders. Growth funds tend to be more volatile in the short-term than income-oriented funds, but they tend to provide better long-term returns.

- **Aggressive growth funds.** There are several types of aggressive growth funds. Some invest in depressed stocks that have turnaround potential. Others look for trendy stocks or startup companies that could blossom into major corporations. And still others invest in potential takeover stocks that could experience a sharp run-up in price. These funds tend to be riskier than growth funds—particularly over the short term—but might provide outstanding returns in a good market.

- **International and global funds**. These funds give investors a stake in the international market. *Global funds* are funds that invest in both U.S. and foreign stocks, whereas *international funds* invest strictly in foreign stocks. Because they invest in foreign stocks, international funds can be somewhat riskier than U.S. growth stock funds. However, by investing in an international fund as part of a diversified portfolio, you add foreign diversification, which actually helps reduce the overall risk of your portfolio.

- **Sector funds**. These specialty funds invest primarily in stocks of a single industrial sector. There are funds for almost any market sector you could name—precious metals, utilities, high-tech, medical technology, and financial services, among others. If you think gas and oil stocks are ready to take off, you might invest in an energy fund. If you want a hedge against inflation, you might invest in a gold fund that buys the stocks of gold mining companies. While specialty funds have broad stock holdings within a specific sector, they lack the diversity and safety of traditional stock funds. If the sector is faring poorly, so will the fund. Tech stock funds were red hot through the 1990s but went into a devastating free-fall when the tech market crashed.

- **Index funds**. Index funds are designed to mirror the overall market. By buying an index fund, you can expect to achieve a return similar to the growth of the overall market. While that might not seem particularly adventuresome, index funds do tend to outperform about 80 percent of all mutual funds, because only about 20 percent of mutual funds beat or exceed the market averages over a period of 5 to 10 years. Some index funds are tied to the Dow Jones Industrials, while others are designed to reflect the Standard and Poor's 500 Index.

WHO SHOULD BUY STOCK FUNDS?

Stock funds are appropriate for conservative, moderate, and aggressive investors interested in capital appreciation or a combination of income and appreciation as part of a diversified portfolio.

Stock fund gains are taxable, however, so the best place for them might be your tax-sheltered retirement plan. But many investors hold stock funds in both their retirement accounts and their personal accounts.

WHO SHOULD *NOT* BUY STOCK FUNDS?

If you need income, very few stock funds can match the income level offered by bond funds and REITs. There are, however, a few funds that focus on dividend-paying stocks.

Very conservative investors who are interested primarily in preservation of capital might steer clear of stocks and stock funds because they are riskier and more volatile than savings bonds, government bonds, and other fixed-income investments. But even conservative investors should have some stocks or stock funds in their portfolio to provide broader diversification. And while stocks and stock funds can be very volatile in the short-term, over the long-term they have outperformed every other conventional type of investment.

RETURN

Mutual fund returns are similar to stock market returns and tend to mirror the ups and downs of the market. But because of fees charged by mutual funds, the average stock mutual fund return slightly trails the performance of the overall market. Since 1925, the stock market has posted an average annual return of 10.7 percent.

The best value for investors would be a no-load fund. No-load funds charge no fee to buy or sell shares of the fund. But even the no-load funds charge annual management fees of about 1 to 2.5 percent, which can be a drag on the fund's total annual return.

If you use a broker to buy a fund, the broker will probably insist on selling you a load fund. Load funds charge about 4 to 8 percent just to buy the fund. Even in a pretty good year in the stock market, that 4-to-8-percent fee can go a long way toward wiping out your first-year gains with the fund. On top of that, load funds (like no-loads) also charge annual management fees of about 1 to 2.5 percent. However, if you buy a load stock fund and hold it for many years, the effects of that initial up-front fee would diminish dramatically over time.

RISKS

Stock funds reduce the risk of owning stocks because they provide broad diversification, with money spread out over scores of different stocks. When you buy individual stocks, if one or two stocks in your portfolio tank, that can have a significant impact on your total return. But if one or two stocks in a mutual fund tank, that would have little impact on the fund's return because the performance of other stocks in the portfolio would compensate for the subpar stocks.

But despite their diversification, stock funds are, in fact, made up of stocks, and stocks can be volatile. During the huge market downturn of 1999 through 2003, virtually every investor in stock mutual funds lost money, and many lost 40 to 70 percent of their invested assets. All that diversification did nothing to stop the hemorrhaging.

That one ugly period of the market, however, tells only a small part of the story. Over the long term, stocks and stock funds go through many up and down cycles. Those same funds that tanked in the early 2000s posted phenomenal gains in the 1990s. Many stock funds were up 100 to 300 percent from 1992 to 1999. With stock funds, you have to take the bad with the good.

Some types of funds are safer than others:

- **Growth and income funds**. These tend to be fairly steady funds because they invest in blue chip stocks that pay dividends (which tend to be relatively steady performers), and might also invest in some bonds, which helps broaden the diversification and reduce the risk.

- **Long-term growth funds.** By investing primarily in blue chip stocks, these funds have only moderate risk. Blue chip stocks—stocks of large, well-established companies—have been among the steadiest performers in the market.

- **Aggressive growth stocks**. These funds take more chances and invest in lesser-known companies in their quest for better returns. In a good market, that can lead to superior performance, but in a down market, these funds tend to be loss leaders.

- **Sector funds.** These funds, by design, are poorly diversified. They buy stocks of a specific sector of the economy. High-tech sector funds were big in the 1990s and provided spectacular returns. But when the tech bubble burst, those same funds had spectacular losses, many dropping 50 to 75 percent.

UPSIDE

In addition to their diversification, stock funds have many benefits, including:

- **Professional management**. Professional investment managers do the work for you.

- **Capital appreciation.** Stock funds strive to provide capital appreciation by investing in stocks with the potential for stock price growth.

- **Income.** Some stock funds focus on dividend-paying stocks, so that investors receive a steady stream of income—and the potential for capital appreciation.

- **Liquidity.** With most funds, you can pull your money out simply by calling the company and telling them to sell your shares.

- **Low investment requirements.** It doesn't take a lot of money to invest in a mutual fund. Initial minimum investment requirements vary from about $250 to $2500 for most funds. And once you're a shareholder, most funds allow you to contribute even smaller subsequent amounts—usually in the range of $50 to $250—so it becomes very easy even for small investors to build a position in a fund.

- **Direct purchases.** You can buy shares directly from the mutual fund company simply by calling the company's toll-free sales line.

- **Checking deduction plans.** With most funds, you can have money automatically withdrawn from your checking account and invested in the fund each month or each quarter.

- **Automatic reinvestment.** With most mutual funds, investors can have their dividends and capital gains distributions automatically reinvested in additional shares of the fund with no additional sales fee.

- **Automatic withdrawal.** Retired investors sometimes opt for withdrawal plans that authorize the fund to pay out a set amount to the investor from his or her fund account each month or each quarter.

DOWNSIDE

Stock funds do have a couple of notable drawbacks, including:

- **Fees.** Annual fees and loads (for the load funds) can cut into your total return.

- **Potential for loss**. Despite their diversification, stock funds are still tied to the stock market and are susceptible to broad swings of fortune.

- **Less control**. If you like to make your own decisions on the types of companies you own, mutual funds might not be for you. They can invest in tobacco companies, defense companies, major polluters, and anything else the fund manager believes could make the fund a buck. You might not like some of the companies you own as a shareholder in the fund.

- **Taxes**. If you buy a stock and hold it for years, the stock can increase in value 100 fold and you would still not owe a dime in taxes as long as you don't sell it. But holding onto your mutual fund shares does not achieve the same purpose. Fund managers do a lot of buying and selling within the fund. If those trades result in a net gain, you would owe taxes on that gain. You would also owe taxes on all dividends paid by the stocks in the fund portfolio (just as you would owe taxes on all dividends paid by an individual stock). One way to avoid the annual taxes of mutual funds is to park your funds in a tax-sheltered retirement account.

HOW TO BUY STOCK FUNDS

You can buy load stock funds through your bank or broker, but if you want a no-load fund, the best way to buy them is through the mutual fund company. You might also be able to buy no-loads through brokers, but you might face an extra fee to compensate the broker.

Load funds come with either front-end or back-end loads. With a front-end load, you pay a fee of about 4 to 8 percent up front when you buy the shares. With a back-end load, you pay the load when you sell the shares. If you hold for several years, the back-end fee is slowly reduced or eliminated entirely after about five or six years.

All mutual fund companies have toll-free numbers you can call to set up an account and get additional information on their funds.

You can find information on mutual fund performance in a number of publications. *Money* magazine, *Baron's, Consumer Reports*, and several other publications offer rankings of hundreds of funds in periodic special editions. Many investment Web sites also have fund rankings.

You can use those rankings to find funds that have had solid returns for many years. Try to find a fund (or funds) that has been among the leaders in total return for the most recent five-year period—and have had good returns on a yearly basis for at least the past five years.

BIGGEST CONCERNS

Before you buy a stock fund, you need to check out its history and management. You want a fund that has been among the leaders in its category for total return and year-to-year consistency.

Once you find a fund with a good track record, make sure the fund manager who established that track record is still with the fund.

Finally, check on fees. If possible, buy a no-load fund instead of a load fund. That will save you a lot of money up front. Then compare annual management fees. There can be a big difference from one fund to another. You might find fees as low as 1 percent or as high as 2.5 percent. A front-end load and a higher management fee can make a difference in your return over the short or the long term.

TIMING

Timing the stock market can be an exercise in futility. Investors have tried with little luck to time the market effectively. The problem is that timing involves a series of buy and sell decisions, and those decisions are based primarily on guesswork. You might guess right on when to sell stocks, but you better guess right again on when to buy them back before the market goes up. Then guess again on when it will go back down, and so forth. But if you guess wrong (and you will eventually, because no one gets it right every time), you could miss out on a huge run-up in the market, or you could buy into the market just as it takes a tumble.

If you do want to try to time the market, conventional wisdom says that when stock prices start to get too high and stock price-to-earnings ratios (PE) get too high, you should lighten up on stock funds and move some money into other investments. But if you jump the gun and start moving assets too early, you can miss an even bigger run-up in prices. In a bull market, stocks often go up higher than expected, and in a bear market, they drop down further than expected. (More on stock market timing in Chapter 24 on Stocks.)

A number of studies have shown that a buy-and-hold approach is the most effective way to invest in stocks and stock funds. Find a good fund and hold onto it for the long term.

One of the most effective ways to invest in stock mutual funds is to use a system known as "dollar cost averaging." With dollar cost averaging, you rely on the volatility of the market to ensure that you automatically buy more shares when stocks are down and fewer shares when stocks are up. You do that by investing exactly the same amount of money every month, automatically, regardless of whether the market is moving up or down.

For example, let's say that you invest $100 a month automatically in shares of an index fund. When the market is high, and shares are trading at, let's say $10, your $100 investment would pay for 10 shares. When the market is low, and shares are trading at, let's say $5 a share, your $100 investment would buy 20 shares. So you are able to buy 10 more shares at the lower price. That's the magic of dollar cost averaging—you automatically buy more shares when stocks are the lowest and fewer shares when stocks are the highest. Best of all, you can do it automatically because mutual fund companies offer automatic deduction plans for investment in their funds, making dollar cost averaging as easy as signing a form. So the process continues to work without any effort on your part.

MONITORING YOUR STOCK FUNDS

You can find information on mutual funds, including price and yield, in business newspapers and all over the Web. *The Wall Street Journal* has a huge special section on thousands of mutual funds every three months. On the Web, *Morningstar.com* and *multexinvestor.com* are two of the best sites for mutual fund information. America Online and Yahoo! also have a wealth of current information on thousands of funds, as do dozens of other financial Web sites, such as *www.allstarStocks.com* and *www.money.cnn.com.*

ASSET ALLOCATION

The amount of money you allocate toward stock mutual funds would depend on your tax situation, your financial situation, your investment goals and your tolerance for risk.

Conservative investors concerned with preservation of capital might want to limit their investment in stocks and stock funds to 20 to 40 percent of assets.

Aggressive investors looking for long-term growth would probably want to put more than 50 percent of their assets in stocks or stock funds because stocks have posted the best average annual returns of any conventional form of investment over the past century. Aggressive investors with a long-term time horizon might want to put up to 60 to 80 percent of assets into stocks. That could lead to a lot of portfolio volatility in the short-term but better than average returns over the long term. Moderate investors might stick with 50 to 70 percent stocks and stock funds to lower the volatility while still aiming for strong long-term growth.

You should also consider diversifying within the stock fund universe. Moderate investors, for instance, might build a stock fund portfolio that would include about 40 to 60 percent blue chip growth funds, 10 to 25 percent growth and income funds, 15 to 25 percent aggressive growth funds, 5 to 15 percent international funds, and 5 to 15 percent sector funds.

SPECIAL CONSIDERATIONS

Most load funds give you the option of choosing either a front-end load (in which you pay a fee of about 4 to 8 percent up front to buy fund shares) or a back-end load (which charges a similar fee when you sell the fund). Selecting the best fee option for you can be very confusing.

With back-end loads, if you hold a fund for several years, the load percentage drops each year that you own the fund. If you hold the fund for six to eight years before you sell, you would probably not have to pay any load at all.

So if you plan to buy a fund and hold it for several years, the obvious choice would be to pick a back-end load fund over a front-end load fund, right?

Wrong.

There is a catch to the back-end load funds that very few investors or brokers are even aware of. Back-end load funds generally charge a significantly higher annual management fee than front-end load funds. Over a period of several years, that additional annual fee can end up costing you more than you would have paid with a front-end load. For instance, the Smith Barney Aggressive Growth Fund Class A shares charges a 5-percent up-front fee and a 1.2-percent annual management fee. Its Class B shares charge no up-front fee but a 5-percent redemption fee and a 2.03-percent annual management fee. So you're paying almost a full percentage point a year in additional management fees to own the back-end load fund. You have to hold the fund for eight years before the back-end fee disappears. By then you've paid an additional 6.4 percent in annual expenses over the Class A front-end load fund. So you would actually spend more money on expenses with the back-end load fund than you would with the front-end load fund.

The best bet, if possible, is to find a good fund with no load and a reasonable annual management fee. That gives you a big head start over either type of load fund.

18

CERTIFICATES OF DEPOSIT (CDS)

Income and safety

PERHAPS THE BEST THING you can say about certificates of deposit is that they typically pay a higher rate of return than a bank savings account. But that's not saying much.

To their credit, CDs are very safe—generally FDIC insured up to $100,000. And they offer some flexibility. You can buy CDs for terms of 30 days (or less) or as long as 10 years (or more), and you can get them in denominations of a few hundred dollars to a hundred thousand dollars.

But among fixed-income investments, this is one of the bottom feeders of the food chain. Even tax-free municipal bonds tend to pay as high a rate as most CDs (which are fully taxable).

But millions of Americans buy CDs because of the convenience, the safety, and the fact that they pay a better yield than a standard bank savings account. CDs, which are available through any bank and most investment companies, are similar to bonds in that they generally pay a fixed rate of return for a fixed period of months or years. You can also buy variable-rate CDs, but most CDs are issued with a fixed rate. CDs with maturities of one year or less generally pay all the interest at maturity, while longer-term CDs pay interest every six months.

WHO SHOULD BUY CDS?

CDs are geared to conservative investors interested in safety and income. More aggressive investors might also be interested in CDs because they can help provide diversification for their portfolio, although there are other fixed-income investments that offer a better return or a tax advantage.

WHO SHOULD *NOT* BUY CDS?

CDs would not be attractive to investors looking for a high level of income or capital appreciation.

RETURN

The returns for CDs vary as market interest rates vary.

The longer the term of the CD, the better the interest rate. You can also get a better return by shopping around for CDs at different banks and financial institutions. By running a search for "certificates of deposit" on the Internet, you can get quotes from banks around the country. In some cases, the difference from one five-year CD to another can be 1 percent or more—a significant difference in a low interest market.

Most CDs with maturities of one year or less pay interest when the CD matures. Those with longer maturities typically pay interest semiannually.

Generally speaking, CDs offer returns similar to T-notes, T-bills, and municipal bonds (without the tax benefits), and somewhat lower than A-grade corporate bonds.

Table 18-1 shows how the returns for CDs compared with other types of fixed income investments is the summer of 2003. The percentages listed are about average for the market

TABLE 18-1

	6 months	1 year	5 years	10 years
CDs	1.35%	1.6 %	2.0 %	3.5%
T-bonds				4.3*
T-notes			2.4*	3.2*
T-bills	0.8*	1.0*		
Municipals	1.0 – 1.4*	1.2 – 1.8*	2.0 - 2.5*	3.0 – 4.5*
Corporate		1.0 –1.5	3.0 – 5.0	4.0 – 6.0
Money market	0.95 (variable)			

* T-bonds, T-bills, T-notes, and municipal bonds all offer tax advantages not offered by CDs

RISKS

Most CDs, if held to maturity, carry very little risk. CDs issued by banks and most investment companies are insured against default for $100,000 per account by the FDIC. If you want to put more than $100,000 into CDs, you may wish to spread out your purchases to different institutions, so that you have up to $100,000 in coverage at each institution.

But be wary of CDs that pay a significantly higher rate than the market average. There's a good chance they are not insured by the FDIC.

UPSIDE

CDs provide several important benefits, including:

- **Steady income.** Long-term CDs offer a steady (semiannual) payout for income-oriented investors.

- **Safety.** CDs are considered very safe, with most CDs insured for up to $100,000 by the FDIC.

- **Liquidity.** There is a secondary market for CDs, although reselling your CD can cut into your return.

- **Convenient.** You can buy CDs through any bank, most investment companies, and on the Internet at many financial services Web sites.

- **Competitive rate.** CDs will not likely make you rich, but the rate they offer is usually better than the normal bank savings account rate and competitive with many other fixed-income investments.

- **Flexible.** You can buy CDs for the short-term (30 days) or the long-term (10 years or more), and you can buy them in denominations of a few hundred dollars, $1000, a few thousand dollars, or as much as $100,000.

DOWNSIDE

CDs have a few drawbacks, including:

- **No tax advantages**. Unlike municipal bonds, which are free of federal taxes, and Treasury issues, which are free of state taxes, CDs are fully taxable at your normal earned income tax rate.

- **Lower returns**. Although their rates are better than a savings account, CDs pay lower rates than you would get with corporate bonds and many REITs. They also offer no capital appreciation potential, and historically have trailed the average annual returns of stocks and stock mutual funds by a wide margin.

- **Tied to low returns**. If you buy a long-term CD during a low-interest cycle, you could be stuck with a low rate while market interest rates move up. If you wanted to sell on the secondary market, you would have to take a loss on the principal because your CD would no longer be worth as much due to its low yield in a higher-yield market.

HOW TO BUY CDS

CDs can be purchased at any bank or savings and loan, and at most investment companies. CDs are also available online at dozens of Web sites (most of which are sponsored by banks). To shop the market, do a search engine search of "certificates of deposit" on the Internet, and you will find dozens of Web sites of institutions offering CDs for sale. It gives you a good opportunity to compare prices between banks on the Web—and your own bank.

CDs are available for the short-term (30 days) or the long-term (10 year or more), and you can buy them in denominations of a few hundred dollars, a few thousand dollars, or as much as $100,000.

Bank CDs tend to pay higher rates than investment company CDs, although that is not always the case.

BIGGEST CONCERNS

Be sure to find out when your CD matures. Your banker may talk you into a CD with a higher rate of return, but what he or she may not focus on is the fact that the higher your return, the longer the term of the CD. You may not want to tie up your money for 5, 10, or even 20 years, so make sure you know when the CD matures before you invest your money.

You should also find out about any penalties for early withdrawal. See how much of a penalty you would be assessed if you cash in your CD early.

Also find out exactly the interest rate you'll receive and how you will be paid—whether it's after the CD matures or semiannually during the life of the CD.

TIMING

The best time to buy CDs, as with nearly any traditional types of fixed income investments, would be during periods of high interest rates. It can be difficult to predict the movement of interest rates, but as interest rates drop, the value of existing CDs increases. Buying CDs near the peak of interest rates would put you in a very strong position. As interest rates drop, you could hold the CD and continue to enjoy high returns, or you could sell the CD on the secondary market at a premium, earning a profit on your investment.

By contrast, the worst time to buy CDs would be during a period when interest rates are low and are beginning to rise. That would put you in the unenviable position of either collecting low rates throughout the term of the bond, or selling it out at a loss. You could opt for CDs with shorter terms, but the shorter the term, the worse the return. One other option would be to buy a variable-rate CD, so if market interest rates move up, your return would go up as well. But when rates are low, you should probably limit your exposure to CDs.

MONITORING YOUR CDS

Unless you buy a variable CD, your CD rate and maturity are not going to change. If you have questions on your CD, refer them to the bank or financial institution that sold you the CD.

ASSET ALLOCATION

The amount of money you allocate toward CDs would depend on your tax situation, your financial situation, your investment goals, and your threshold for risk.

Conservative investors who are more concerned with preservation of spending power than they are with growth might want to invest 20 to 60 percent of their assets in fixed-income assets such as CDs, T-bonds, corporate bonds, and bond mutual funds. You might want to lighten the weighting of CDs in the portfolio during periods of low interest rates, and increase the weighting during periods of high interest.

Aggressive investors looking for long-term growth would probably want to limit their investment in CDs (and most other fixed-income investments), particularly in times of low interest. However, an allocation of 5 to 20 percent of assets in CDs and other fixed-income investments even for aggressive investors would help provide balance and diversification, and could buoy the portfolio when stocks are down. But, unless you put it in a tax-deferred retirement account, interest on your CD is fully taxable. If you're in a high tax bracket, you might opt instead for a municipal bond or fund.

SPECIAL CONSIDERATIONS

Some CDs can be "called" or terminated if the issuer wants to get out from under a high rate. If you buy CDs during a high interest cycle, and rates begin to fall, there's a good chance the issuing institution will recall the CD and refund your money. That leaves you with a load of cash and a lower interest rate environment in which to invest it. If you buy a long-term CD with a high rate, make sure you buy one that can not be recalled by the issuer.

19

UNIT INVESTMENT TRUSTS

Income or Appreciation, Low Fees, and Diversification

A UNIT INVESTMENT TRUST (UIT) is much like a mutual fund, giving small investors a share in a diversified pool of investments, but without the annual management expenses. UITs were first introduced in the 1960s as a way to allow small investors to own tax-exempt municipal bonds. Now there are also UITs for stocks, corporate bonds, government bonds, and other types of investments. In all, there are about one million unit investment trusts on the market, although that number fluctuates constantly.

Unlike mutual funds, which are actively managed by a professional portfolio manager, unit investment trusts are basically unmanaged. The UIT sponsor sets up a portfolio of stocks or bonds in a trust, then sells shares in the trust to investors. Once the UIT is formed and shares are sold, no more changes are made in the portfolio, and the sponsor turns the trust over to a trustee (usually a bank or brokerage company). The trustee is in charge of safekeeping and of sending out bond disbursements or stock dividends to UIT shareholders. When the bonds in the UIT mature, the principal is returned to shareholders and the UIT is closed.

In the case of a stock UIT, provisions are made in the charter to sell out the stocks at a specific time—usually at the end of one year. The proceeds are then sent out to shareholders and the UIT is closed. Usually investors are given a renewal option so that they can be included in a new UIT offering launched by the same sponsor when the previous UIT expires.

By contrast, mutual funds are considered "open-ended" with no termination date. As long as the funds have enough shareholders to stay afloat, they continue to operate. Many funds have been around for decades.

One of the biggest advantages of UITs is the fee structure. Although UITs do charge an up-front fee that can be similar to a load mutual fund, they have very low annual maintenance fees of about 15 to 20 basis points (0.15 to 0.2 percent) compared with a typical mutual fund annual management fee of about 1 to 2.5 percent.

For bond investors, one of the biggest advantages of UITs is that you don't have to worry about fluctuations in bond prices. With bond funds, as market interest rates rise, the value of the bonds in the fund—and the fund shares themselves—decline in price. But because bonds in UITs are generally held to maturity, temporary fluctuation in the market price of the bonds is irrelevant—unless you sell out early.

WHO SHOULD BUY UNIT INVESTMENT TRUSTS?

UITs are appropriate for income-oriented investors who want to earn a steady income with a minimum of risk. They are also suitable for aggressive stock-oriented investors looking for capital appreciation. Because of their small minimum requirements—usually about $1000—UITs are ideal for small individual investors.

UITs have also been very popular with affluent investors looking for tax-exempt income because many UITs specialize in tax-exempt municipal bonds.

WHO SHOULD *NOT* BUY UITS?

If you like to make your own decisions on your investments, you might not be interested in a UIT. Or if you prefer to be invested in a mutual fund that is actively managed, you might want to steer away from UITs.

Otherwise, there is a wide range of UITs geared to investors with vastly different goals and risk thresholds.

RETURN

UITs are similar in return to the markets their investments represent. Bond UITs offer returns similar to bonds, and stock UITs offer returns similar to the stock market. The annual maintenance fee is so small it has little impact on the return of the UIT.

However, UITs do have front-end fees of about 1 to 5 percent, which can have a small drag on performance, although the impact would be minimal for investors who hold the UIT for several years.

RISKS

Like mutual funds, UITs provide excellent diversification for stock or bond investors. Instead of relying on the performance of a single stock or bond, UITs spread the risk over a broad range of securities. If one stock tanks or one bond defaults, the UIT is still buoyed by the other investments in the portfolio.

Bond investors might find UITs preferable to mutual funds because UITs are less volatile and more predictable. Fluctuations in interest rates affect the market price of the bonds within a mutual fund. In a rising interest environment, you can actually lose money in a government bond fund (or any bond fund). When interest rates rise, bond values drop. A 2-percent rise in market interest rates can push the value of a bond fund down by 10 percent or more. (Conversely, when market rates fall, bond fund prices appreciate.) That's why bond funds can be riskier than the bonds themselves.

But with UITs, bonds are held to maturity so you don't have to worry about fluctuations in market prices. Once the bonds mature, you get your principal back in full, and the UIT is closed.

UPSIDE

UITs have many benefits, including:

- **Diversification.** UITs have a broad portfolio of stocks or bonds, providing excellent diversification while lowering the risks.

- **Income.** Bond UITs pay a yield similar to the type of bonds they hold, ranging from low-yielding government bonds to high-yielding junk bond funds. Many stock UITs also provide income through dividends, and might experience capital appreciation if the stocks in the trust increase in price.

- **Liquidity.** You have an option of selling your UIT shares back to the sponsoring company if you don't want to hold them through to the end of the term.

- **Low investment requirements.** It doesn't take a lot of money to invest in a UIT. Many have minimum investment requirements of about $1000.

- **Appreciation potential**. Stock mutual funds can increase in value if interest rates decline.

- **Muni UITs are tax-free**. If you own a UIT made up of municipal bonds from your state, your interest payments would be free of federal taxes, and in many cases, state and local taxes, as well.

- **Low maintenance fee**. Once you own a UIT, your annual expenses are minimal—much lower than a mutual fund.

DOWNSIDE

UITs have a few drawbacks, including:

- **Up-front fee.** To buy shares of a UIT you must pay an up-front fee similar to a load mutual fund, although many UITs have sales fees considerably lower than load funds.

- **No active management.** Unlike a mutual fund, UITs are not managed. Once the sponsor puts the portfolio together, that is how it stays until the UIT is closed and initial investments are returned to shareholders.

- **Potential for loss**. Stock-based UITs can fall in value in a bad stock market.

HOW TO BUY UNIT INVESTMENT TRUSTS

You must buy UITs through a sponsoring dealer-broker. The cost is usually about 1 percent (sometimes less) to 5 percent. They are usually available in minimums of about $1000. You can resell the UIT to the same broker-dealer who sold it to you. There is usually no redemption fee, although the amount you receive for your shares will depend on the current value of the investments within the fund.

Many bond UITs have terms of 20 to 30 years, although some come in terms of 10 years or less. A few even come with terms of under a year.

Most stock UITs have very short terms—usually about a year—although many of those UITs offer investors an annual renewal option so that their money will be automatically reinvested in a stock-based UIT for as many years as they wish.

BIGGEST CONCERNS

Before you buy a UIT, learn what you can about the sponsor. Find out about the success of other UITs offered by the same sponsor. You want a sponsor with a solid track record.

Be aware that UITs are not actively managed, although that shouldn't be a problem for most bond UITs. Investors in stock UITs might be a little more nervous about the lack of management, although stock UITs usually have very short terms, at which time the sponsor liquidates the UIT and builds a new portfolio for investors interested in renewing.

TIMING

The same factors that would guide an investor to buy or sell a stock or bond apply to UITs. For instance, the best time to buy a bond UIT is when interest rates are high because you get a good return and, if rates start to drop, the value of the bonds within the UIT go up. The worst time to buy would be when interest rates are low.

MONITORING YOUR UITS

With about one million UITs on the market, there is not a central source you can find to get information on every UIT. To find out how your UIT is doing, check your statement or call the broker who sold you the UIT.

ASSET ALLOCATION

The amount of money you allocate toward UITs would be similar to the asset allocation you would use for individual bonds or stocks or mutual funds.

SPECIAL CONSIDERATIONS

If you wish, you can buy a UIT for your tax-sheltered retirement plan. Stock or bond UITs might be appropriate for your account, depending on your goals and threshold for risk. But you wouldn't want to buy a municipal bond UIT for your retirement fund because those bonds are already tax-exempt.

20

HEDGE FUNDS

Capital Appreciation-Oriented,
High Risk, or Risk-Averse

O NCE AN OBSCURE CONCEPT embraced by a very small slice of the investing public, hedge funds have grown in popularity in recent years because of their ability to provide positive returns even when the stock market is heading lower. There are now nearly 7000 hedge funds on the market, although most are fairly small compared with the assets of traditional open-end mutual funds.

Hedge funds are unregulated investment trusts that use a variety of sophisticated techniques to play the market, such as stock options, leveraging, arbitrage, derivative securities, and long and short stock positions. While the strategies—and the returns—of different hedge funds vary widely, the primary aim of most hedge funds is to reduce volatility and risk while attempting to provide positive returns and preserve capital under all types of market conditions.

But don't grab your change purse yet. Unless you can show that you have at least $1 million in investment assets—not including equity in your home—you wouldn't be allowed to invest in most hedge funds. They have strict requirements because of the risks associated with hedging techniques. The bylaws of most hedge funds stipulate that they must have fewer than 100 investors, and those investors must have a minimum of $1 million in investment assets.

However, because of the growing demand for hedge funds, some alternative options have been introduced recently that require assets of only $100,000 to $250,000. In fact, a few new hedge funds that meet stricter reporting and disclosure guidelines have received approval from the Securities and Exchange Commission to accept an unlimited number of investors, with lower investment requirements. Shareholders must still meet certain net-worth requirements, but minimum investments are as low as $25,000.

The mutual fund industry has also jumped on the hedge fund wagon, introducing a handful of funds that mimic the hedging techniques used by hedge funds, such as short-selling and leveraging. However, because those mutual funds are regulated by the Securities and Exchange Commission, they must adhere to tighter restrictions on short-selling, leveraging, and other hedging issues that can affect the safety of the fund. Some of those mutual funds have minimums as low as $2000. The improving cost of admission for hedge funds might ultimately earn hedge funds a more universal acceptance among individual investor investors, but for now, the vast majority of hedge fund assets comes from pension funds, insurance companies, and other institutional investors.

There are many types of hedge funds, with their own unique strategies, goals, and hedging techniques. Here are some of the most common types of hedge funds:

- **Stock selection**. Combines long and short stock positions. In other words, it buys stocks (that's the long position) and then it buys stock options that increase in value if the market drops (that's the "short" position). The aim is to profit from both overvalued and undervalued stocks in the market. While these funds offer the potential for strong gains, they can be volatile and risky.

- **Aggressive growth**. Buys stocks that are expected to experience increasing earnings. Often focuses on smaller emerging stocks and specialized sectors such as technology or biotech. Often hedges by buying short options positions in stocks that are expected to have disappointing financial results. These funds can be very risky with high volatility.

- **Directional trading**. Trading is based on speculation in the direction of the market for multiple asset classes, such as stocks and bonds. Managers use both model-based systems and subjective evaluation to make buying and selling decisions. These funds are often volatile.

- **Relative value**. Trading is based on spread relationships between pricing components of financial assets. Managers often use leveraging to increase returns, but market risk is kept to a minimum.

- **Distressed securities**. Invests in stocks and bonds of financially distressed companies, buying them at deep discounts. Investment risk is considered moderate.

- **Macroglobal**. These funds try to profit from changes in global economies, buying and selling equities, bonds, currencies, and commodities from around the world in order to take advantage of changes in those markets. They typically use leveraging and derivatives to attempt to enhance returns. These funds can be very volatile.

- **Short selling**. These funds focus on selling securities short, in expectation of making a profit if the securities decline in value. Risk and volatility is considered very high.

- **Market neutral**. There are two kinds of market neutral hedge funds. Some use arbitrage to hedge out most market risk by taking offsetting positions—often buying different securities of the same issuers. For instance, they might be long in a company stock, but short in its convertible bonds. This off-setting strategy typically results in low volatility. The other market neutral approach uses securities hedging, investing almost equally in long and short positions of stocks in the same market sectors. Most use leveraging to increase performance. The counterbalancing approach can limit total return, but it also keeps risk and volatility at minimum.

- **Special situations**. These funds invest in companies that are involved in mergers, hostile takeovers, reorganizations, and leveraged buyouts. They hope to buy at distressed prices and sell after a recovery. They often employ heavy leveraging to take advantage of timely opportunities. They also leverage through the purchase of derivatives in order to hedge market risk and keep volatility to a moderate level.

FUNDS OF FUNDS

One approach that is gaining in popularity is the fund-of-funds approach, in which a fund manager buys shares of a pool of different hedge funds. Studies have shown that while the performance of individual hedge funds can vary dramatically, with excessive gains and losses in any given year, funds that invest in a pool of 20 or so different hedge funds tend to provide a very stable, steady return. The volatility of the fund-of-funds hedge funds is usually quite low, particularly for those funds that make an effort to include a mix of hedge funds that reflect counterbalancing strategies.

The one drawback to the fund of funds is that you face a double layer of management fees. You are charged all the applicable fees for the funds within the fund, and you must pay an additional fee to compensate the manager of the fund of funds. But the benefits of owning a pool of hedge funds can be well worth the extra expense.

WHO SHOULD BUY HEDGE FUNDS?

Hedge funds are geared to affluent, sophisticated investors who are seeking capital appreciation and are willing to take some risks. They can also be used to provide balance and diversification for a broad investment portfolio. Some hedge funds serve as an excellent counterbalance to stocks, increasing in value as the stock market declines. Aggressive investors might find some hedge funds that offer the potential for a higher return than the stock market averages, although those funds typically carry a higher risk. Less aggressive investors might prefer a fund of hedge funds where the money is spread around to several different types of funds to provide balance, diversification, and greater safety.

WHO SHOULD *NOT* BUY HEDGE FUNDS?

Because of their perceived risks, many hedge funds are open only to investors who can prove that they have substantial investable assets. In most cases that would be $1 million in assets over and above your home equity. That doesn't mean you have to invest $1 million—you just have to prove that you have it. Other funds might require assets of $100,000 to $250,000, and a few have lowered their investment minimums to $25,000.

Most hedge funds offer no current income (or very little), so they would not be appropriate for income-oriented investors. Nor would they be suitable for smaller investors, new investors, risk-averse investors, or conservative investors who are more comfortable with traditional investments—unless the hedge funds were used to provide diversification for a broader portfolio.

RETURN

Over the past two decades, hedge funds as a group have produced returns very similar to stocks, although the returns of hedge funds on an individual basis have varied dramatically from fund to fund and year to year. No one fund or type of fund seems to dominate the hedge fund market. They all take their turns near the top and the bottom, according to a recent study by Morgan Stanley Dean Witter. The study reported that the annualized geometric return of all hedge funds from 1990 to 2000 was 18.9 percent.

But while the long-term returns of stocks and hedge funds are similar, the path can be quite different. Because of their hedging strategies, many hedge funds trail the overall market when stocks are booming and far exceed the market when stocks are in decline. For example, during a recent 15-year period, the Standard & Poor's 500 Index had 15 negative quarters, totaling a negative return of 108.1 percent. During those negative quarters, the average U.S. equity mutual fund had a total negative return of 111.8 percent, while the average hedge fund had a total negative return of only 9.2 percent. On the other hand, during the market's 15 best quarters, stocks would have significantly outperformed most hedge funds. Hedge funds invest heavily in short options and derivatives, which keep them going in a down market but cost them money in an up market.

RISKS

Hedge funds run the gamut from very safe and steady to high–risk, high–return, high volatility. However, many investors use hedge funds to lower their total portfolio risk by buying hedge funds that are designed to perform well when stocks are down.

For a relatively safe investment, you might consider a market neutral fund that uses counterbalancing long and short positions to minimize volatility. But safety does have a price. While that approach works wonders in a down market, it can impede the growth of the portfolio in an up market.

Another good choice for low risk, solid return, and instant diversification would be a fund of funds. Because of their vastly different strategies and techniques, hedge funds show very little correlation in performance— particularly from different categories of hedge funds. According to the Morgan Stanley Dean Witter study, pooling a representative sample of all of these strategies into a single fund or index lowers the risk and volatility while still achieving solid returns.

UPSIDE

Hedge fund advocates say that one of their advantages is their flexibility because they are not subject to SEC regulations. They are able to buy speculative investments and use financial instruments and investment techniques unavailable to normal mutual funds. That flexibility, including the use of hedging strategies to protect against downside risk, can make hedge funds less volatile. But that same flexibility can also lead some fund managers to higher risk and greater volatility—it's all in how the manager runs the fund.
Hedge funds can offer several benefits:

- **High returns**. Hedge funds, on average, provide about the same annual returns as stocks.

- **Can help lower risk**. Because the returns of many hedge funds are not correlated with the stock market, they can provide a boost to the portfolio when the stock market is down.

- **More stable returns for fund of funds.** If you own a fund of hedge funds that invests in a pool of hedge funds, you can expect more stable returns under most market conditions than you would get with stocks or individual hedge funds.

DOWNSIDE

Hedge funds have a number of drawbacks. Volatility is perhaps the biggest drawback for most funds, but there are other disadvantages, as well:

- **High cost of admission**. Most individual investors could not afford to buy hedge funds because of the asset requirements and the minimum investment requirements.

- **High risk**. Many funds offer the potential for high return, but with it comes a very high level of risk and volatility.

- **Lack of liquidity.** Most hedge funds are private partnerships with fewer than 100 investors. While there is a secondary market for hedge funds, it is not as well organized as stock and bond markets. Finding a buyer for your shares could be a problem.

- **Lack of diversification.** Unless you buy a fund of funds, most hedge funds focus on a very narrow aspect of the investment market.

HOW TO BUY HEDGE FUNDS

You might be able to buy hedge funds through your broker, but not necessarily. Hedge funds are not as accessible as normal mutual funds. You might need to contact a hedge fund company to make your purchase. Then you must qualify financially. Most require that you have assets of at least $1 million in addition to your home equity.

Typically, hedge funds charge a fee of about 1 percent of assets invested, plus 20 percent of the profits—which they would only collect in years when the fund is profitable. The fee structure encourages the fund managers to stretch their performance, although that's easier said than done.

Recently, some hedge funds have begun to require smaller assets—$100,000 to $250,000. A couple of leaders in that market include JLH Capital Investment and Gryphon Partners. A new, more closely regulated generation of hedge funds is available with minimums of just $25,000. UBS PaineWebber is the leader in that market.

Finally, there are a handful of mutual funds that use the long-short hedging strategies characteristic of hedge funds. They require a minimum investment in the range of just $2000. Leaders in that market include the Merger Fund and Calamos Market Neutral Fund.

You can find more information on the hedge fund market at *www.hedgefund.net*.

BIGGEST CONCERNS

The biggest concern for many speculative hedge funds is the enormous loss you could take if the fund manager makes the wrong choices. Many hedge funds take a make-or-break approach, using heavy leveraging and speculative investments in quest of a big payoff. But if the manager guesses wrong, the fund could suffer heavy losses. Not all hedge funds are high risk, but for those in the high-risk realm, the volatility and potential for loss can be enormous.

TIMING

Because of their high costs and relative lack of liquidity, hedge funds don't provide an easy opportunity to time the market. But with most funds, timing shouldn't be an issue. In fact, the whole point of many hedge funds is to provide steady returns in every type of market, so that you don't have to worry about market timing.

But there are many specialty funds that do better under certain conditions. If you're an aggressive investor, in a high stock market, you might want a fund that bets heavily on the short side; when the market is low, you might want a leveraged fund that is heavy on the long side. The best idea, however, might be to pick a fund with a good track record or a fund of funds and let the professional manager worry about the timing of the investments.

MONITORING HEDGE FUNDS

Hedge fund investors receive a regular statement from the fund, providing an update of the fund's price and performance.

Because hedge funds are typically small private investment trusts, they don't receive much coverage in the business press, although that is starting to change as some financial publications devote more of their space to hedge funds.

One of the best sources of information on hedge funds is the Web site *www.hedgefund.net*. The site provides a free database of hedge fund information and performance statistics on more than 2300 hedge funds. Another site that offers information on hedge funds is *www.hedgefund.assn.org*.

ASSET ALLOCATION

Hedge funds offer asset allocation benefits because they have separate growth trends from stocks, bonds, and other types of investments. This lack of correlation works well in terms of balancing out the performance of a portfolio, while still providing a relatively high long-term rate of return.

However, hedge funds currently are geared primarily to more affluent, sophisticated investors. They are not an essential element of a diversified portfolio. But they could bring some solid diversification benefits to an aggressive, capital appreciation-oriented portfolio. As hedge funds become more affordable, they might become a more common portfolio component for individual investors.

SPECIAL CONSIDERATIONS

According to a study by Morgan Stanley Dean Witter, since 1990, the youngest hedge funds (less than one-year track record) have clearly out-performed the older funds, particularly on a risk-adjusted basis. So in selecting a hedge fund, track record is not as important as you might expect. The younger, smaller funds tend to do better than the older estab-lished funds—perhaps because of their flexibility.

21

COLLECTIBLES

Entertaining but Unpredictable

I F YOU WANT TO INVEST in collectibles, you have many, many choices. But be sure to pick something you enjoy, because unless you're better or luckier than most, you could find collecting to be a lot of effort with a little reward.

My experience with collectibles might be typical of many who have delved into the world of stamps, coins, sports cards, memorabilia, autographs, rare books, comic books, dolls, art, antiques, crystal, or any of the endless array of collectibles.

When my father was a boy in the 1920s, he had a paper route. He had one customer who always paid him with old Indian head pennies from the late 1800s. My dad saved the pennies throughout his childhood and for most of his life. When I was growing up, he had them hidden away in his closet on a shelf above his hanging clothes. One day a burglar broke into our house and stole the coins. The insurance company paid us face value for them—about $8—although they were worth hundreds of dollars as a collection.

I, too, had a paper route when I was a boy. I set aside some of my earnings each month to buy stamps for a collection, expecting that later in life the value of those stamps would grow to represent a small fortune. The rest of my money I spent on candy or baseball cards. I had thousands of baseball cards, including some boxes of cards my next door neighbor gave me that dated back to the 1940s. At the time, baseball cards were simply considered child's play. No one thought of them as collectors' items.

When I moved away from home, my dad threw out my baseball cards and held onto my stamps.

I wish he had thrown out the stamps and saved the baseball cards.

In the 1980s baseball cards suddenly became popular with collectors, and the value of those early cards skyrocketed. My collection would have been worth tens of thousands of dollars.

My stamp collection, on the other hand, has grown in value at a snail's pace. All the money I poured into it from my paper route and the hundreds of hours I spent sorting through those stamps has yielded very little in value.

But one day, a year or so ago, I noticed a large box on the kitchen table that had come in the mail. I asked my wife about it, and she said, "Oh, that's just some old stamps from my late uncle in Ohio. They've been sitting up in my father's attic for years. I don't think they're worth much." Based on my own philatelic experience, I concurred. But once I opened the box, I was awestruck by the collection this man had put together. There were hundreds of four-stamp plate blocks from the 1930s and 1940s in mint condition. There were dozen of entire pages of unused stamps in mint condition, with 50 stamps to a page. There was a small stack of first day issues. There was even a stamped envelope from the first trans-Atlantic flight of the Hindenburg and another from the first trans-Pacific flight of the Boeing Clipper. With mounting excitement, I dug through that collection for hours, staying up until 4 a.m. I was convinced that this new collection would make me forget the disappointment I had experienced with my own collection.

The next day I went straight to Barnes & Noble and bought the latest edition of the Bookman Stamps and Covers Price Guide. I couldn't wait to see what those stamps were really worth. But as I began to page through the catalog checking on the market value of the stamps, I was flabbergasted to find that most of those mint blocks of four were worth only 20 to 30 cents. The mint sheets of 50 were worth only $20 to $30. The entire collection that had my jaw dropping the night before looked to be worth only about $3000 or so—and dealers would probably offer even less. After all those years— seven decades in all—those stamps were still barely worth the paper they were printed on.

I estimated that, in all, the uncle had invested around $1000 in his entire stamp collection, which was a pretty good sum in those days. If he had put that money into the stock market instead of stamps, how would he have fared? Here's the sad news: In the early 1930s when he began collecting stamps, the Dow Jones Industrial Average was at about 60 points. In recent years, it has been in the range of 8000 to 10000 points. That means the market grew about 150 fold during that roughly 70-year period. If the uncle had put his $1000 investment into the broad stock market instead of stamps, his investment by now would have grown to about $150,000—a far cry from the roughly $3000 the stamp collection is worth.

Moral of the story: Collect for fun because there is no guarantee your collectibles will ever hit the jackpot. Dealers and professional collectors can make money in the collectibles market, but that's usually at the expense of the casual collector.

Collecting is really more of a hobby than an investment. In fact, in some cases, it's more like a second job. Antique automobile collectors, for instance, put in long hours keeping their cars maintained. You need adequate storage facilities, you need insurance, and you need a knack for buying the right items at the right price. And acquiring that knack can take years—at great expense.

Liquidity is another big problem of the collectible's market. If you want to actively buy and sell as a collector, you might need to work a booth at collectibles shows, go on eBay, advertise in trade publications, and use other resources to hawk your goods. That's not investing that's work—unless you love it. Then it's probably worth the effort. Otherwise, you might be better served to stick with stocks, bonds, REITs, and mutual funds. They're a lot easier to buy, hold, or sell, and, most likely, a lot more profitable for you, as well.

OIL AND GAS INVESTMENTS

Income and Capital Appreciation with Some Risk

N O ONE QUESTIONS the future importance of oil and gas or the potential for profits in the oil and gas industry. But actually getting a piece of that profit has proven difficult for investors.

The price of oil experienced a huge jump in the 1970s from about $2 a barrel in 1973 to as much as $35 a barrel in 1981. Investors have been waiting for the next big leap ever since. They're still waiting. Oil prices in recent years have fluctuated from about $18 to about $35 a barrel, with an average price of around $28. With prices like that, it's difficult to get the U.S. domestic oil production industry off the ground. They simply can't produce oil inexpensively enough here to compete with oil fields elsewhere, including the Middle East, Russia, Canada, and Argentina.

In the 1980s, oil and gas limited partnerships were very popular because they offered tax-free income. But tax law changes cut the benefits of investing in oil and gas partnerships, and the stagnant price of oil kept profits to a minimum. The partnership boom of the 1980s has slowed to a trickle. There are still some investment companies that offer partnership opportunities, but they have not been particularly popular or rewarding. There are many more opportunities in Canada where the tax laws are much more favorable for partnership investment.

There are three other ways to buy a stake in the oil industry:

- Oil and gas stocks. There are many oil and gas companies on the stock market involved in a wide range of operations, including drilling, pipelines, and production. ExxonMobile, ChevronTexaco, and British Petroleum are among the leading corporations involved in the oil industry. But there are dozens of other publicly traded companies involved in oil and gas operations, such as Apache Corp., Dynergy Energy Partners, and Chesapeake Energy Corp.

- Energy mutual funds. There are a number of sector funds that focus exclusively on energy stocks.

- Oil and gas futures. For sophisticated investors, you can buy options on energy futures contracts—whether you think prices are heading up or dropping back. If you buy options based on rising prices, and you guess right, you can make a quick profit with a relatively small investment. But if prices stay about the same or drop down, you lose 100 percent of your investment. If you think oil or gas prices are heading down, you can buy options based on that, so if prices do drop, you'll earn a profit. This is a very risky form of short-term investing, based primarily on guesswork. Oil and gas futures are not appropriate for most investors.

WHO SHOULD BUY OIL AND GAS INVESTMENTS?

Whether it is through stocks, funds, or a limited partnership, energy industry investments can add diversification to any portfolio and serve as a hedge against inflation.

If you're interested in income, there are a number of companies in the energy industry that pay very good dividends. For instance, Kinder Morgan Energy Partners, which operates more than 10,000 miles of petroleum pipelines and more than 10,000 miles of natural gas pipelines, has paid a dividend of about 7 to 9 percent in recent years.

Oil and gas stocks and funds also offer capital appreciation potential. In a strong energy market, if earnings and revenue are moving up, stock prices and energy fund prices should move up as well.

WHO SHOULD *NOT* BUY OIL AND GAS INVESTMENTS?

Beginning investors with a small portfolio wouldn't necessarily need to add specific oil and gas investments to the portfolio. But advanced investors should probably include at least a small investment in energy stocks or funds in the portfolio.

Energy limited partnerships and energy futures are both risky investments that would not be appropriate for the vast majority of individual investors.

RETURN

Oil and gas stocks and mutual funds have provided returns similar to other stocks, although they tend to move in different cycles from the rest of the market. They tend to do very well when the energy market is in turmoil, but may drop back when things stabilize.

The high dividends (6 to 10 percent in some cases) offered by some energy services and pipeline companies are among the best of any sector of the stock market. In addition to the dividends, those stocks also offer the potential for capital appreciation.

RISKS

The risks are similar to risks with other types of stocks and funds. When the gas and oil market becomes overstocked, prices can slide quickly. Energy investments can stay in a depressed state for months at a time, but they always seem to bounce back because oil-producing countries ultimately adjust their output to compensate for the oversupply.

UPSIDE

Oil and gas investments offer a few strong benefits:

- **Capital appreciation.** In a strong energy market, you can enjoy excellent growth of your oil and gas stocks, mutual funds, or limited partnership shares.

- **Income.** A number of oil and gas stocks and funds pay high dividends.

- **Inflation hedge.** Oil and gas investments can serve as a hedge against inflation and a hedge against international turmoil. Oil prices tend to go up in times of inflation and uncertainty.

DOWNSIDE

Oil and gas, like all stocks and mutual funds, have some risks and drawbacks. In a slow market—and there are many with oil and gas—you may see your shares take a tumble. Income and capital gains from your oil and gas investments are fully taxable.

If you're interested in a limited partnership, they are few and far between, so the opportunities are limited. But one of the reasons these investments are scarce is because they really haven't performed well in recent years, so there is little demand. And like all limited partnerships, there is essentially no liquidity. Once you're a shareholder, you may be expected to hold for 7 to 10 years.

HOW TO INVEST IN OIL AND GAS

Investing in oil and gas stocks and mutual funds is as simple as buying stocks or mutual funds. (See chapters on stocks and stock mutual funds.) If you're interested in a limited partnership, you will need to ask your broker. If your broker can't help you, you may need to call around to other major investment firms to see if they have any partnership opportunities.

BIGGEST CONCERNS

The biggest concern with energy investments is the potential oversupply of gas and oil. When energy markets get overstocked, profits fall quickly, and that can cause a sharp drop in oil and gas prices on the commodities market. On the other hand, energy shortages can cause prices to spike, which can mean big profits for oil futures investors.

Oil and gas stocks don't react quite the same to changes in the supply, but they do move a little. In a strong economy, when gas and oil use is up, energy stocks do very well, but they can slump when the economy is slumping and demand for energy is in decline.

TIMING

As difficult as it may be, the best time to buy oil and gas stocks and mutual funds is when demand has been down and those stocks have been in a slump. That's when you can buy them at a good price. Ideally, you should load up on energy stocks just as demand is beginning to return. But if you load up when demand is picking up, you better be sure to lighten up when demand declines. That goes for related stocks, as well. For instance, Astropower, which makes solar energy products, was trading at about $9 a share in early 2000, but as oil shortages brought more interest in alternative energy sources, Astropower soared to $40 a share. In 2001 and the first half of 2002, it traded in the range of about $20 to $35. But it made a steady descent to under $10 a share as interest in alternative energy sources diminished.

The only pure short-term play in the oil sector would be futures trading. Stocks, funds, and limited partnerships move much more slowly. To actually bet on short-term hikes or declines in oil prices—for instance, oil is at $25 a barrel and you expect it to go to $30—you would need to buy options on oil futures. That's a very complex, difficult, and risky type of investing. A better word for it might be "gambling." The vast majority of investors would be better served to invest the traditional way through stocks and funds. With patience, you will enjoy some growth and income with those investments.

MONITORING YOUR OIL AND GAS INVESTMENTS

You can follow oil and gas stocks and mutual funds in the business press or at dozens of leading financial sites on the Internet. If you own a limited partnership, you'll have to rely on your broker to keep you up-to-date on the investment.

ASSET ALLOCATION

Oil and gas investments are not an absolute "must" for every portfolio, but they can be an important part of an asset allocation mix. Whether it's a stock, fund, or limited partnership, an investment in energy should help diversify your portfolio and give you a strong position in the portfolio during times of international turmoil (when energy stocks tend to do the best) while other stocks in the portfolio are suffering.

If you look at the future of oil and energy, it appears obvious that that sector will continue to be very important for years to come. But because of the volatility of the energy sector, you may not want to put too much of your assets in oil. Oil stocks, mutual funds, and limited partnership shares should probably constitute no more than 5 to 10 percent of your portfolio.

SPECIAL CONSIDERATIONS

Some recent reports by oil industry experts suggest that oil could become increasingly scarce in future years, which would help the performance of U.S. domestic producers and increase profits for energy investors. Dr. Collin J. Campbell, who has studied the oil industry for the past 45 years, recently reported that oil discovery may be on the decline, and that oil shortages could begin to crop up by 2008. He says that Norway, which is the world's second largest oil exporter, is expected to see its production decline by 50 percent by 2006 because of declining reserves.

Roger Blanchard of Northern Kentucky University concurs with Campbell's assessment. "The rapid decline of major fields appears to exist in many producing basins around the world and must be considered in long-term supply forecasts. If this situation isn't recognized by national and international organizations that make projections of long-term supply, the future may present some unpleasant surprises." Oil and gas shortages around the world would pump up stock prices of domestic drilling, production, and service companies. Exactly when that will happen is still uncertain, but the long-term outlook for investors is definitely promising.

C H A P T E R

23

PRECIOUS METALS
Inflation Hedge, Slow Growth

NOTHING GLITTERS LIKE GOLD, but that doesn't necessarily make it a great investment. Investors have been buying gold, silver, and platinum for centuries, with occasional short-term success, but over the long term, precious metals have been one of the worst investments on the market.

The best time to buy precious metals is when inflation appears to be picking up or when world events cast an uncertain shadow on the future of global stability. But in normal times, precious metals, as an investment, typically go nowhere.

Precious metals had their biggest day in the sun in 1980 when the price of an ounce of gold went from about $200 to a peak of $887.50 during a tempestuous period in the Middle East. Gold prices have not come close since. Gold has been trading primarily in the range of about $250 to $400 an ounce ever since.

There are several ways to invest in precious metals:

- **Physical ownership**. You can buy gold bullion in sizes ranging from one-ounce ingots to 400-Troy ounce gold bars. Or you can buy certain gold coins, such as the South African Krugerrand, the Canadian Maple Leaf, or U.S. Eagle coins. You can also buy silver and platinum in various forms.

- **Certificates**. Some banks, dealers, and brokers offer warehouse receipts that represent ownership of precious metals that are held in safekeeping.

- **Mining stocks.** There are a number of mining stocks, primarily in South Africa, that you can buy on the New York Stock Exchange. Those stocks tend to rise and fall in sync with fluctuations in the price of precious metals. Some pay a small dividend, but all have had flat share price growth for many years.

- **Mutual funds**. There are a number of mutual funds that invest in gold and precious metal stocks. Like the precious metal stocks, those funds have shown an occasional bounce, but they've gone nowhere over the long term.

- **Commodity futures and options.** You can buy gold on the commodities or options markets, but those investments are geared to well-capitalized investors with an expertise in the market.

The biggest problem with precious metals is that they do not represent a working investment. When you own stock, you own a share of a company that has an entire force of employees working to provide products or services that turn a profit. As a shareholder, you participate in that profit. But precious metals just sit there. Their value either goes up or down depending on outside economic factors, but they produce nothing—no income, no profits.

All that glitters is not gold, and even gold can lack some luster as an investment—unless you buy and sell it at just the right time.

WHO SHOULD BUY PRECIOUS METALS?

Precious metals are appropriate for advanced investors interested in hedging against inflation and economic uncertainty. They can be profitable to short-term oriented investors who buy at the right time (just as the threat of inflation or economic uncertainty hits) and sell at the right time (when the threat of inflation or economic uncertainty ends).

WHO SHOULD *NOT* BUY PRECIOUS METALS?

Precious metals are of no interest to investors who want income or investors who want capital appreciation. In fact, there is really very little reason for any long-term individual investor to invest in precious metals.

RETURN

Precious metal investments provide some temporary appreciation when they're hot, but they tend to drop back down to previous levels when market interest diminishes.

For the past 20 years, they have provided almost no appreciation at all. After reaching its peak at $887.50 an ounce in 1980, gold has never regained that level. It has traded in the range of about $200 to $400 an ounce ever since.

Precious metal stocks and mutual funds have also been flat long-term performers with some occasional bursts of volatility. For instance, from 1993 to 2003, the precious metals mutual fund category was down an average of about 0.4 percent per year, according to Morningstar Investment Research. Mining stocks have produced about the same return for that 10-year period.

Owning gold bullion or other precious metals tends to be even less profitable than stocks and funds because you have to pay high premiums to purchase the metals, safekeeping, and insurance costs to hold them, and sales taxes.

RISKS

Precious metals are very volatile. You'll never lose all of your money with a precious metals investment, but you could see a sharp decline.

There is one more risk with precious metals—unscrupulous dealers. Be careful who you buy precious metals from because there have been a number of precious metal scams over the past few decades.

UPSIDE

Precious metals have several benefits, including:

- **Inflation hedge.** Precious metals rise in value with inflation or in periods of economic uncertainty.

- **Diversification.** In a portfolio of other investments, precious metals can help buoy the portfolio when other investments such as stocks and bonds are doing poorly.

- **Many options.** There are several ways to buy precious metals, including physical possession, certificates, stocks, mutual funds, or futures or options.

DOWNSIDE

Precious metals have some notable drawbacks, including:

- **Problems of physical ownership.** If you own gold coins, gold bars, or other precious metals in the physical form, you face high premiums to buy and sell, sales taxes, and safekeeping and insurance costs. Owning precious metals is a lot different than owning a stock or bond.

- **Low returns.** In whatever form, precious metals have proven to provide very low returns. In fact, for the past 20 years, they have provided almost no appreciation and, with the exception of some small dividends paid by some mining stocks, they offer no income.

- **Potential for loss**. If you buy at the wrong time, you could take a loss on your precious metal investments.

HOW TO BUY PRECIOUS METAL INVESTMENTS

Precious metals are available through various dealers and brokers at a wide price range. Coins and certificates can be purchased through major banks. There are fees to buy and sell precious metals. Certificates can cost 3 percent or more in commissions plus storage and insurance fees. Certificates usually come in minimum denominations of $1000.

Gold stocks and mutual funds are available through brokers and mutual fund companies, with the usual commissions, loads, and management fees (see Stock Mutual Funds or Bond Mutual Funds).

Professional traders and advanced investors often use options and futures to invest in precious metals. If you anticipate a run-up in gold prices, for instance, you can buy an option on gold contracts at the current price, and if gold prices go up, you earn a profit on that jump in price. But if prices drop or hold steady, you lose the cost of your option when it expires.

BIGGEST CONCERNS

As an investment, precious metals offer no income and very little in the way of long-term appreciation. While bonds pay income and stocks tend to appreciate in value over time, precious metals tend to move up in times of uncertainty and back down when that uncertainty diminishes. Aside from some periodic ups and downs, gold prices have been relatively stagnant for two decades. That's why gold and other types of precious metals would not be an appropriate investment to include in your long-term retirement portfolio.

TIMING

The best time to buy precious metals is at the very outset of inflationary fears or concerns over global stability, war, or economic crisis. Precious metals often go up in price as oil prices go up, or as disruptions in the Middle East fuel fears of rising oil prices.

But when tensions ease, or inflation or oil prices stabilize, be ready to unload immediately because the price of precious metals could drop quickly.

MONITORING PRECIOUS METALS

For updates on the price of precious metal stocks or mutual funds, you can check the major financial publications or any of hundreds of financial Web sites that offer stock and fund information. The Value Line Investment Survey also covers several mining stocks.

For additional information on precious metal investments, such as gold bullion, there are several Web sites that offer information and market prices, including *www.financialsense.com/metals/main.htm*, and *www.the-privateer.com/gold.html*.

ASSET ALLOCATION

In times of economic uncertainty or anticipated inflation, investors might want to allocate a small percentage (5 to 10 percent) of assets to precious metals investments, but they are not generally considered a key component of a balanced portfolio. In fact, for long-term investors, precious metals can be dead weight in the portfolio because they can trade in roughly the same range for years If you want a hedge against inflation, instead of precious metals, you might consider an I-Bond or a TIPS. I Bonds are like savings bonds that grow in value at a quicker rate if inflation picks up, and TIPS are similar to T-bonds, except that they have a variable interest rate that rises if inflation picks up. (See chapters on I-Bonds and TIPS.)

24

STOCKS

Capital Appreciation, Income,
Diversification, and Risk

FOR ALL THEIR VOLATILITY AND UNCERTAINTY, for all the toil and trouble they caused investors in recent years, stocks have actually been excellent long-term performers. In fact, for the past century, no other investment covered in this book has topped stocks.

Stocks can provide income, capital appreciation, and diversification. They can give you a position in all the leading industries. Oil, gold, financial services, retail, automotive, medical, foods, transportation, corporate services—you name it, you can build a position in it in the stock market.

When you buy a stock, you become a part owner in a corporation. If you own shares of Microsoft, for instance, then Bill Gates works for you. When you're a shareholder in a company, as that company's fortunes rise, so will the value of your shares. But if the company's business sours and the sales plummet, your shares will dive in sync. Fortunately, over the long term, stocks have generally enjoyed positive returns. But the risk is ever present.

Stocks are traded on one of several exchanges, including the New York Stock Exchange, the American Stock Exchange, the NASDAQ market (which is similar to an exchange), and the over-the-counter market used by the very smallest, newest companies.

You can buy or sell stocks any business day through any brokerage company, including full-service brokers, such as Merrill Lynch, discount brokers, and online brokerage companies. The market for stocks is very liquid.

There are several categories of stocks. You can build a very diversified portfolio including income as well as capital appreciation across a broad range of industries. Here are the leading types of stocks:

- **Blue chips**. Also known as large capitalization stocks, blue chips are typically well-known companies that are leaders in their industries, such as IBM, GM, Johnson & Johnson, and Wells Fargo. They are considered the safest stocks, although even blue chips can go through major market fluctuations. Blue chips generally pay dividends.

- **Small capitalization stocks.** These tend to be smaller, newer companies on the way up. Many will struggle, particularly in a slow economy, but a few will break through and post outstanding returns, helping propel the stock price to new highs. On average, small stocks have outperformed blue chips by almost 2 percent per year over the past 70 years. But averages can be deceiving. You're definitely taking more chances with smaller stocks.

- **Midcap stocks**. These are stocks of midsized companies on the way up. They are not household names like the blue chips, but they are larger and more established than the small-cap stocks. They typically have slightly better growth potential than the blue chips, but not quite the home run potential of small stocks.

- **Income stocks.** Stocks that pay good dividends are referred to as income stocks. Utility stocks, such as gas and electric companies, are among the favorites of income stock investors. Like most income-oriented stocks, utility stocks don't offer much capital appreciation potential, but they do pay excellent dividends, and those dividends tend to go up a little bit each year. A well-diversified portfolio should have both growth and income stocks. Retired individuals often increase their portion of income stocks to provide additional income to supplement their other retirement income. In addition to utilities, other types of stocks that tend to pay the best dividends would include banks, insurance companies, certain investment companies, tobacco stocks, REITs, and energy services companies. As a point of comparison, in recent years, most blue chip stocks were paying dividends of about 1 to 2 percent, banks were paying savings account interest rates of about 2 percent, and the better-yielding income stocks were paying dividends of about 3 to 10 percent.

- **Foreign stocks.** A number of major foreign stocks also trade in the United States on the New York Stock Exchange and other markets. Nearly 1000 foreign stocks trade here as "American Depository Receipts" (ADRs). By buying stocks from outside the United States, you spread your risks and become less reliant on the U.S. economy. However, an easier way to invest in foreign stocks—and the preferred way for most investors—would be to buy an international stock mutual fund.

- **Preferred stock.** Preferred stock is similar to a bond in that it pays a fixed dividend that is set when the stock is issued. Not to be confused with convertible securities, preferred stocks do not offer much price appreciation potential, nor do they raise their dividends from year to year as many common stocks do. The one advantage of preferred stock is that, should the company be liquidated, preferred shareholders would have claims satisfied before common shareholders. However, preferred stock is not an investment that would be suitable for most investors.

- **Value stocks.** Value investors look for bargains in the stock market— stocks they consider to be undervalued compared with the rest of the stocks in the market. There are value stocks of every size and industry. The key for value investors is finding stocks that are trading at a very low price relative to the value of their assets or their earnings. Value investors take some chances buying low-priced stocks that the market has shunned in hopes that those stocks will soon find favor in the market and begin moving up.

- **New issues.** Known as IPOs (initial public offerings), new issues are one of the riskiest areas of the stock market. New issues tend to be very speculative because they often have new products or services that are still earning market share. New issues can enjoy explosive growth, but there are many more busts than booms in the IPO market.

- **Cyclical stocks**. Some industries do better during specific stages of the economy, such as automakers, paper, chemical, steel, and aluminum manufacturers. Because they face high fixed costs of operation, these companies do best when the economy is strong, and their production engine is at full tilt. But they suffer when the economy slows down because they still face high costs due to the overhead of factories, machinery, and a large workforce. The best time to buy cyclical stocks is at the bottom of a recession when their price is down and their earnings are down but no longer declining. The best time to sell a cyclical stock is during an economic expansion when the company is producing at full capacity. After that, there is little room for further growth. And once the economy hits the next phase—the slowdown—the stock price could decline.

WHO SHOULD BUY STOCKS?

Stocks or stock mutual funds are appropriate for nearly any type of investor, although some investors may prefer a larger allocation of stocks than others. Aggressive investors looking for capital appreciation would use stocks to boost their total return.

Income investors may prefer income stocks that not only pay dividends, but also typically hike those dividends each year. That's the biggest advantage income stocks have over most types of bonds.

Conservative investors may want to keep a much smaller allotment of stocks in their portfolio, but they should still have some stock investments as part of a diversified portfolio.

Stock gains and dividends are taxable, however, so you might want to do as much of your stock investing as possible in a tax-sheltered retirement plan.

WHO SHOULD *NOT* BUY STOCK?

Investors interested strictly in a place to park some money for the short term should not consider stocks.

For long-term investors, the vast majority should have a stake in the stock market, but individual stocks may not be the best choice for many investors. The better choice might be stock mutual funds because their diversification and professional management make them a safer, more convenient option.

Stocks (or stock mutual funds) may seem a little too risky for very conservative investors interested in preservation of capital or income. However, because of the superior long-term performance of stocks, even very conservative investors should consider holding at least a small portion of stocks in their portfolios because of the diversification benefits and the potential boost to their long-term performance.

RETURN

Although the only certainty stocks offer is the certainty of volatility, over the long term they have been the best-performing conventional form of investment.

Since 1925, the stock market has posted an average annual return of 10.7 percent. Small stocks have done even better, with an average annual return of about 12.5 percent.

If you're investing for income, dividend-paying stocks in recent years have offered yields of about 2 to 8 percent.

Figure 24-1 illustrates the comparison in long-term performance between stocks and other types of investments.

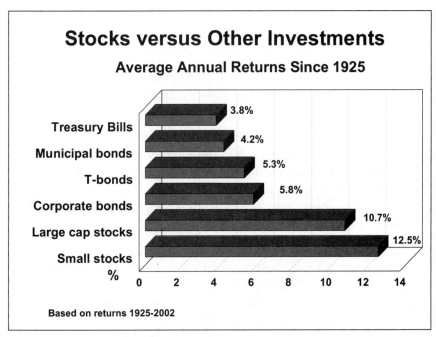

FIGURE 24-1

RISKS

All stocks carry risks, and the risks can be extreme. During the tech-market meltdown, many stocks went from over $100 a share to a few cents a share. That's an extreme example, but it illustrates that the risks in the stock market are real. And the risks don't all come from start-up tech stocks. Enron was one of the world's largest corporations when it nosedived into bankruptcy, costing its shareholders billions of dollars. K-mart is another long-established company that went into bankruptcy recently.

That's why diversification is so important in stock investing. You can reduce your risks by spreading your money around to several different stocks from several different industries.

In fairness, tech stocks and Enron do not give a true reflection of the market's risk. They are the exceptions. There are hundreds of stocks, such as 3M, Wrigley, Anheuser-Busch, Merck, and Coca-Cola, to name a few, that have enjoyed excellent growth for many decades and have increased their dividends every year for decades.

UPSIDE

Stocks offer many benefits for investors, including:

- **Capital appreciation.** Stocks offer the best potential for growth of any conventional form of investment. As the company grows and expands, the stock price should grow with it.

- **Income.** Many stocks offer excellent dividends. In fact, some stocks pay dividends that are higher than the returns you would get from T-bills or T-bonds. While dividend-paying stocks do carry the same risk of loss of appreciation typical of all stocks, they can (and often do) increase in value. With a bond or bank account, there is no appreciation—just the annual interest.

- **Increasing stream of income.** Unlike bonds that pay a fixed rate from inception to maturity, most dividend-paying stocks raise their dividends year after year. For investors who rely on dividends for much of their income, that increasing stream of income serves as an excellent hedge against inflation. In fact, it's not unusual for a company to raise its dividend for 10 to 20 consecutive years or more. That dividend payment can serve as a hedge against inflation. The longer you own the stock, the higher the dividend you'll receive—as long as the company continues to be profitable.

- **Liquidity.** Stocks can be bought or sold all day every business day.

- **Low investment requirements.** There was a time when investors needed to buy stocks in relatively large blocks because brokerage commissions were in the range of $75 to $100 per trade for relatively small orders. But now, with online trading commissions of only a few dollars a trade, you can economically buy a few hundred dollars worth of stock (or a few thousand) without the commissions becoming a drag on your total return. Many companies also offer something known as a dividend reinvestment and stock purchase plan (DRIP) in which you can buy shares of stock directly from the company commission free.

- **Checking deduction and automatic reinvestment plans.** DRIP plans give investors the option of having money withdrawn automatically each month to invest in stocks, and they allow investors to have their dividends automatically reinvested in additional shares of stock.

- **Tax-free growth.** As long as you hold onto a stock and do not sell—even if it grows 100-fold—you would owe no taxes on the appreciation. You would, however, owe taxes on any dividends you receive, and you would owe capital gains taxes on your gains once you sell the stock.

DOWNSIDE

Stocks have a few notable drawbacks, including:

- **Potential for loss.** Despite the impressive long-term averages, stocks can lose value. Despite diversification, stock funds are still tied to the stock market and are susceptible to broad swings of fortune.

- **Lack of diversification.** Individual stocks are very narrowly focused—one company in one industry. In order to achieve proper diversification, you may need to invest in 10 to 20 different stocks across several different industries or in a handful of stock mutual funds.

- **Taxes on dividends**. You owe state, local, and federal income taxes on all dividends you receive from stocks (unless they are in a tax-sheltered retirement fund).

- **Taxes on capital gains**. Although you pay no taxes on price gains of the stocks you own, if you sell those stocks for a profit, you would owe income taxes on the gains. On the other hand, if you have losses on stocks you sell, you would get to claim those losses for a deduction on your income taxes.

HOW TO BUY STOCKS

You can buy stocks through a full-service broker, such as Merrill Lynch, through a discount broker, or through an online broker such as Ameritrade.

Full-service brokers, who offer you recommendations and research, will charge you about $75 to $100 a trade for smaller trades. Discount brokers, who offer no recommendations or research but simply execute your order, generally charge in the range of $35 to $50 for smaller trades.

Online brokers typically charge a flat fee per trade regardless of the size of the order. That flat fee can vary from firm to firm, from as low as about $5 per order to as high as $25 or $30 an order. So if you plan to buy online, you might want to shop around first for a firm with a low fee structure.

BIGGEST CONCERNS

Diversification is probably the biggest concern you face when you invest in individual stocks. The smaller, less diverse your portfolio, the more volatile it is likely to be.

If you are a new investor, you might start your stock-investing program by buying shares in a broad-based mutual fund. That would provide you with instant diversification.

But many advanced investors build their own diversified portfolios. You can't start with a full portfolio, but you can build it up over time. You might want to start with two or three blue chip stocks and slowly add some other stocks from other industries. The ultimate goal should be to have a portfolio of 10 to 12 blue chip stocks covering a wide range of solid industries. But just because you are diversified doesn't mean the weighting from industry to industry has to be identical. You might invest more in faster growing stocks or industries, such as the medical industry. (See more on stock selection under "Special Considerations.")

Once you have a solid portfolio of blue chips, you might want to add some small and midcap stocks or mutual funds to provide you with greater diversification—and the potential for even higher long-term returns. Finally, you might want to add a few shares of a foreign stock mutual fund to further broaden your diversification.

TIMING

It is virtually impossible to successfully time the market on an ongoing basis. You might be successful at buying a stock or putting money into the market at the right time and the perfect level on occasion. But no one can do that consistently because timing the market involves a series of buy and sell decisions, and those decisions are based primarily on guesswork and emotion. And that can be a deadly combination in the stock market. Market timers run into several problems—they pull their money out of the market too soon and miss a further run-up in prices, or they fail to get back into the market before it rebounds and miss a strong up-tick. Or they get back into the market too soon at a level they believe to be the bottom of the market, only to see stocks drop even further.

Rather than to try to time the market, you should allocate an appropriate portion of your assets to stocks and build a balanced portfolio designed to grow with the market over a period of many years.

If you do want to try to time the market, conventional wisdom says that when stock prices start to get too high and stock price-to-earnings ratios (PE) get too high, you should lighten up on stocks or stock funds and move some money into other investments. But if you jump the gun and start moving assets too early, you can miss an even bigger run-up in prices. In a bull market, stocks often go up higher than expected, and in a bear market, they drop down further than expected.

A number of studies have shown that a buy-and-hold approach is the most effective way to invest in stocks and stock funds. Find some good stocks or funds and build a position in them for the long term.

MONITORING YOUR STOCKS

You can find daily information on stocks, including price and dividend yield, in business newspapers and all over the Web. Your brokerage firm may also send you monthly or quarterly statements, which will detail your holdings and offer current prices.

If you have an online account, you should be able to pull up current price information on your entire account anytime you want.

The best single source of detailed stock research is the Value Line Investment Survey, which offers analysis and long-term financial histories of nearly 2000 of the nation's leading blue chip stocks. Value Line is available at many public libraries. You can also buy a subscription for about $600 a year, or you can get a three-month trial subscription for $65. For more information, go to *www.valueline.com* or call 1-800-654-0508.

If you want to use the Internet to track stocks or do research, there are a number of excellent Web sites available. Here are some of the best:

BusinessWeek Online. Produced by Business Week and Standard and Poor's, this site offers timely market information, a wealth of articles on business and the markets, and research on individual stocks for investors. The stock information includes current quotes, historical quotes, analysts' estimates, insider trading, in-depth profiles, 6-year financial reports, and other stock data and graphs. Go to <*www.businessweek.com*>

CNBC online. Offered in conjunction with Microsoft's MSN.com, this site offers lots of information on stocks and the market, including the standard quotes, charts, financial histories, and earnings estimates. It also offers one other excellent feature—a stock rating summary that includes a rating and brief analysis of the stock, with a pro and con breakdown, and a short-term outlook analysis. Go to <*moneycentral.msn.com*>

CNNMoney. From the editors of CNN and *Money* magazine, this site provides information on the markets and individual companies, including an excellent "snapshot" of each company's stock performance and financial ratios (from Market Guide). It also provides access to articles in *Money*, and many other articles on the business, the market, and the economy. Go to <*money.cnn.com*>

Hoover's Online. Includes in-depth data on more than 10,000 public and private companies, including financial performance, news, Web addresses, and corporate profiles. However, much of the best information is available only to subscribers. <*www.hoovers.com*>

MultexInvestor. This is one of the best free sites on the Web for in-depth research. It has a snapshot report on all stocks that includes current stock price, 52-week highs and lows, dividend information, current ratio, quick ratio, return on equity, return on assets, return on investment, book value, price-earnings ratio, price-to-sales ratio, and other key measures. Go to <*www.multexinvestor.com*>

Quicken.com. One of this best features at this site is its stock analysis section that includes a "One click scorecard" and a "Stock Evaluator" that provide a detailed analysis of each stock, including ratings for revenue growth, income growth, cash flow, return on equity, price-earnings ratios, and other measures. It also provides analysis of growth trends, financial health, management performance, and intrinsic value, and features a chart that shows if the stock's current price is in the recommended "buy" range. Go to *<www.quicken.com>*

Yahoo!Finance.com. This site offers market news and research, message boards, custom portfolios, and a great depth of research on every stock. Go to *<finance.yahoo.com>*

Other good sites include:

- *Allstarstocks.com*, which offers stock quotes, financial information, news, market updates, stock screening, educational articles, model portfolios, original articles by Gene Walden, and links to all of the top investment sites mentioned here. (*allstarstocks.com*)

- *Bloomberg.com*, which contains information on business, market news, market trends, stocks, bonds, mutual funds and economics, as well as original columns by Bloomberg writers. Go to *<www.bloomberg.com>*

- *CBS MarketWatch*, which provides stock quotes and other market information, and has an excellent stock-screening tool. Go to *<cbs.marketwatch.com>*

- *InvestorGuide* (*www.investorguide.com*), which includes information on investing and well-organized links to hundreds of other investment Web sites.

- *Gazebo* (*www.gazebo.com*), which offers preselected portfolios geared to both bull and bear markets.

- *WebFN*, which presents live, online television programming covering the market and investment issues with a steady lineup of top national experts (including regular appearances by Gene Walden) from 8 a.m. to 8 p.m. EST. (*www.webfn.com*)

- *Fool.com*, the Internet home of investing's Motley Fool. (*www.fool.com*)

- *Morningstar.com*, which offers comprehensive research for both stocks and mutual funds that offers some free information and some subscription services.

- *MSCI.com* (operated by Morgan Stanley Dean Witter), the top site on the Web for information on the foreign stock markets—includes up-to-date performance data on all foreign markets, including both the major markets and the emerging markets. (*www.msci.com*)

- *Reuters.com*, which offers excellent market and business news and some financial information on stocks. Go to *www.reuters.com*

- *SmartMoney.com*, which provides detailed information on each stock, as well as stories on business, the economy, and the stock market. Go to <*www.smartmoney.c*om>

- *Wall Street City*, which has articles on business, the economy and the market and a great deal of information and tables on individual stocks. Also provides historical stock quotes. Go to *www.wallstreetcity.com*

ASSET ALLOCATION

The amount of money you allocate toward stocks would depend on your tax situation, your financial situation, your investment goals, and your threshold for risk.

Conservative investors concerned with preservation of capital might want to limit their investment in stocks and stock funds to 20 to 40 percent of assets.

Aggressive investors looking for long-term growth would probably want to put more than 50 percent of their assets in stocks or stock funds because stocks have posted the best average annual returns of any conventional form of investment over the past century. Aggressive investors with a long-term time horizon might want to put up to 60 to 80 percent of assets into stocks. That could lead to a lot of portfolio volatility in the short-term but better than average returns over the long-term. Moderate investors might want to stick with 50 to 65 percent stocks and stock funds to lower the volatility while still aiming for strong long-term growth.

You should also consider diversifying within the stock universe. Moderate investors, for instance, might build a stock fund portfolio that would include about 40 to 60 percent blue chip growth stocks or funds, 15 to 30 percent small and midrange stocks or funds, 10 to 30 percent dividend-oriented stocks, and 5 to 10 percent international stocks or funds.

SPECIAL CONSIDERATIONS

With more than 10,000 stocks on the market, you can be very choosy in selecting stocks for your portfolio. Before you buy, look over a wide selection of stocks, and choose only the very strongest for your portfolio. Or as Winston Churchill once put it: "I'm always satisfied with the very best."

What makes a stock great? Different investors have different standards. Some prefer rundown stocks that look undervalued, others favor small, young companies with untapped potential, while others make most of their buys based on the latest hot tip from their broker, their barber, or their brother-in-law. Value stocks, small stocks, and hot-tip stocks may all have a place in a well-diversified portfolio. But when you're putting together an investment portfolio for the long term, you should build with quality stocks that fit together—not a collection of hard-luck bargains and unproven gambles.

When building your portfolio, you should look for companies that are leaders in their industries, with a long track record of steady growth.

You can use the resources listed above (under "Monitoring Your Stocks") to research stocks for your portfolio. Here are some factors to consider in narrowing down your choices:

- **Earnings growth.** Look for a company that has had earnings growth of 10 to 20 percent per year for the past 5 consecutive years and at least 8 of the past 10 years

- **Solid earnings momentum.** Is the company's earnings growth still going strong, or is it beginning to fade? Check out the most recent quarterly earnings figures and see if the company is still on a strong pace.

- **Revenue growth.** Is the company's sales revenue growth still going strong? Once sales start to slump, earnings may soon follow. You want a company that shows good, steady, long-term sales growth as well as earnings growth.

- **Dividend growth.** Does the company raise its dividend each year? An ever-rising dividend is one mark of a strong company. It also means that your stream of income will continue to rise, combating the effects of inflation.

- **Strong industry.** Is the company in an industry that has been among the strongest, fastest-growing sectors over the past decade or two? Sector strength may not be evident over the short-term (a year or two), but the strongest sectors do show solid strength over a longer period. Some of the strongest industries in the past two or three decades have included medical and pharmaceutical, foods, retail, banking and financial, energy, chemicals and coatings, corporate services, computer technology, telecommunications, packaging, and manufacturing.

Once you've built a blue chip portfolio with a selection of stocks with solid earnings, revenue and dividend growth in the strongest industry groups, you might want to start adding some other types of stocks to your portfolio. The occasional value stock, small stock, or even a hot tip from your friend or broker might be worth taking a chance on, but only as a small part of a well-diversified portfolio.

There are a number of ratios and formulas you can use to decide the best time to buy a stock, but a better approach might be to decide which stocks you want to own, and slowly build a position in those stocks through a regular periodic investment plan. Studies have shown that trying to time your stock purchases has little impact on your long-term success. The important thing is to continue to invest in your key stocks on a regular basis through good times and bad.

WHEN TO SELL

No matter how vigilante you are in selecting quality stocks for your portfolio, you will undoubtedly make some mistakes, or pick some stocks that ultimately hit their peak and start to fade. At some point, you might decide to sell some of your picks and reload with other more promising stocks.

Every few months, you should review your portfolio and evaluate the performance of each of your stocks. Hold onto the ones that are growing, and take a close look at the ones that are lagging. Just because a stock is lagging the market, doesn't make it a "sell." In fact, in a truly diversified portfolio, you should expect to have some stocks that do well while others are faltering. That's part of the point of diversification.

But there are a few good reasons to consider selling a stock:

- **Doesn't meet your expectations**. You bought the stock based on a hot tip from your broker. A year later, it hasn't done anything. You bought it because you expected a quick run-up, and that didn't happen. Time to move it out of your portfolio to make room for a different stock that might be a better fit.

- **No longer meets your standards**. You bought a stock because the company had explosive earnings and revenue growth. Now the earnings have stopped growing and the revenue has slowed to a trickle. That's a good reason to unload the stock. Or perhaps you bought a stock because it was the leading company in its sector. Now a young upstart competitor has begun stealing market share in that sector. That may be a time to sell your stock and start buying shares in the other company. Or you bought a stock because its stock price and price-earnings ratio seemed especially low. Now after a run-up in the stock price, the P/E doesn't seem like the bargain you once had. You bought the stock because it was underpriced. Now that you've made some money and the stock is no longer underpriced, it may be time to sell.

- **Sell when news is grim.** If a stock you own becomes involved in a scandal, comes under legal siege, or becomes involved in a disaster, health issue, or other public controversy, take your lumps and get out as fast as possible. Quick, decisive action could save you a lot of money. Take for example the case of Enron, the Houston-based natural gas and electricity conglomerate that was caught cooking its books. Until the scandal, Enron was the country's seventh-biggest company in terms of annual revenue. When news began to surface that Enron had helped keep billions of dollars in debt off its books through questionable partnerships, the stock was trading at around $60 a share. Over the next six months, the stock steadily dropped from $60 to $40 to $20 to $10. Finally, after the company appeared headed for bankruptcy, the stock quickly sank to under $1 a share. Investors who got out early saved thousands of dollars. Don't ride a questionable stock down. Bail out quickly when news is grim.

- **Sell when earnings drop.** Investment professionals sometimes call it the "cockroach theory." When you see one disappointing earnings report, that may mean more bad periods loom around the corner—just as the sight of a single cockroach usually means that other bugs are hiding in the cupboards. Money managers who follow the cockroach theory like to get out of a stock at the first sign of trouble—even if it means taking a small loss—to avoid taking a bigger loss later should the bad news continue. On the other hand, if this is a blue chip stock with a long history, selling after the first sign of disappointing earnings may be a mistake. But if the bad news continues, don't hesitate to pull the plug. There are plenty of other promising stocks on the market that would fit nicely into your portfolio.

Investing in stocks can help you achieve your lifelong financial goals, but the journey will no doubt be filled with many highs and lows. Hang on for the long-term, and your persistence will ultimately pay off. Or as Charles Kettering once put it, "No one would ever have crossed the ocean if he could have gotten off the ship in the storm."

25

ALLOCATING YOUR ASSETS

TIMING THE INVESTMENT MARKET is a lot like going to a party. If you're buying stocks, for instance, you don't want to be the first one at the party, nor the last to leave. You want to get there just as some of the early guests are arriving, then stick around until a few guests are starting to move toward the door. That's when you grab your coat and head for the next hot spot.

That would be assest allocation at its best. Unfortunately, no one is quite perceptive enough to move adeptly from party to party without some missteps. That's why it's important to spread your assets across a broad range of investments. Asset allocation and diversification might not lead you to the maximum possible total return, but it can help you avoid the type of portfolio meltdown that many tech-stock investors experienced in recent years. Asset allocation can bring you smoother, steadier, safer investment returns.

You might be able to get an edge up on the market if you can make some subtle shifts in the weighting of your portfolio to coincide with movements in the economic cycle. The economy typically goes through five different economic cycles, each with its own investment characteristics. You wouldn't want to make all your buying and selling decisions based on the economic cycles alone, but by understanding the effect they can have on stocks and other investments, you might be able to tweak your asset allocation from time to time to improve your performance.

Here are the five phases of a typical business cycle, and the types of investments that tend to perform the best in each cycle:

1. **Recession.** This slow period in the economy is characterized by falling production, peaking inflation, and weakened consumer confidence. Although it never seems like it at the time, recessions are usually a good time to buy cyclical stocks (such as automakers, paper companies, and other heavy manufacturers). Their earnings might be flat, and their stock prices might be floundering, but they are among the first stocks to take off when the economy turns around. Long-term bonds are also a good bet in a recession because the government tends to lower interest rates to help spur the economy. As interest rates go down, bond prices go up.

2. **Recovery**. Hope begins to emerge. Recoveries are marked by stimulatory economic polices, falling inflation, and increasing consumer confidence. They are a good time to buy stocks, long-term bonds, commodities, oil and gas, and even precious metals to hedge against a possible up-tick in inflation. Smaller emerging growth stocks might do especially well during a recovery, and cyclical stocks should still have some growth left. Real estate also does well during a recovery.

3. **Early upswing.** Once the recovery period passes, consumer confidence is up and the economy is gaining some momentum. The early upswing is probably the healthiest period of the cycle because economic growth can continue without any signs of overheating or sharply higher inflation. Generally speaking, consumers are prepared to borrow and spend more, and businesses—facing increased capacity use–begin investing in plant or office expansion. Unemployment falls, but inflation might pick up. Higher operating levels allow many businesses to cut unit costs and increase margins and profits. The stock market should remain strong, while commodities will continue to rise modestly. The early upswing stage could last for several years. Real estate should continue to do well, but unload the cyclical stocks, because their growth is probably over.

4. **Late upswing**. It's hard to distinguish between the early upswing and the late upswing. But you need to look for subtle signs. The economic boom is in full swing. Manufacturing capacity utilization is at or near a peak. Stocks are rallying, and unemployment is falling. Real estate prices and rents move up strongly, prompting a construction boom.

Inflation picks up as wages increase in the wake of labor shortages. With interest rates rising, bonds become less attractive. In fact, the overall stock market might hit a lull. But commodity prices should continue to rise, bolstered by a huge demand for raw goods to keep the manufacturing boom going.

5. **Economic slowdown**. Once the economy has gone through its recovery and upswing cycles, it's time for a nap. Economic activity starts to slip. Short-term interest rates move up sharply, peaking as confidence drops. The slowdown is exacerbated by the inventory correction as companies, suddenly fearing recession, try to reduce their inventory levels. Manufacturing capacity utilization begins to drop while wages continue to rise, resulting in increasing inflation. In the markets, bond yields top out and start to fall. The stock market might fall, perhaps significantly, with interest-sensitive stocks such as utilities faring the best. Commodity prices might also begin to decline. It might be time to load up on long-term bonds, which rise as interest rates drop.

ASSET ALLOCATION SCENARIOS

What should be in your portfolio? That depends on your age, risk tolerance, personal financial situation, investment goals, the current economic circumstances—and, perhaps, most importantly, how well you want to sleep at night.

Some aggressive investment advisors recommend that stocks constitute as much as 95 to 100 percent of an investor's portfolio because of the superior long-term track record of stocks over other types of investments. Wall Street researchers have done numerous studies on asset allocation theory, with bell curve charts and asset charts and risk-return graphs. Basically what they show is for pure performance, the longer the time frame, the heavier the weighting in stocks, the better the total return. But maximum total return should not necessarily be your goal. Safety should have a role in your portfolio, as well. Stock growth might look great on the charts, but not all stocks meet the averages. As we learned in the tech-stock meltdown, investing in the wrong stocks can have a devastating effect on your portfolio.

That's where asset allocation comes in. Following are some asset allocation scenarios designed to give you some ideas on putting together your own portfolio.

INVESTING FOR GROWTH

Ages: 20 to 39. Stocks and stock mutual funds or stock unit investment trusts should dominate your portfolio, comprising 50 to 80 percent of your investment assets. To balance out the portfolio, look for other high-return investments from different asset classes. For instance, REITs or real estate limited partnerships would be a good place to park 10 to 20 percent of your assets. You might also put 10 to 20 percent in high-yielding junk bond funds or UITs, mortgage-backed securities, and convertible bonds. They all offer above average returns while providing additional diversification for your portfolio.

Ages 40 to 50. Your time horizon to retirement is still long enough that stocks should continue to be a crucial part of your portfolio. If you're still investing for growth—as most people are in the 40 to 50 age range—you should stay aggressive. Stocks could comprise as much as 50 to 75 percent of your portfolio. REITs and real estate limited partnerships could account for 10 to 20 percent, and junk bond funds or UITs, mortgage-backed securities, convertible bonds, and other high-yielding income investments (or zero-coupon securities) could also account for 10 to 20 percent of your assets. However, getting a little more conservative as you get older, you might opt for some slightly more conservative assets, such as corporate bonds, STRIPS, TIPS, or a bond UIT or mutual fund.

Ages 50 to 60. Your time horizon before retirement is shrinking, so you should consider taking a slightly more conservative approach. But, remember, it might only be a few years before you retire, but it could be many decades before you die. You need to maintain a portfolio that will continue to grow for many years after you retire. Stocks should still be a key component, comprising 40 to 70 percent of your assets. REITs and real estate limited partnerships could account for 10 to 30 percent, and fixed income investments could account for 25 to 50 percent. If possible, keep a broad range of fixed-income investments, including junk bond funds or UITs, mortgage-backed securities, convertible bonds, zero-coupon securities, investment-grade corporate bonds and funds, savings bonds, STRIPS, TIPS, and I-bonds.

Age 60 to retirement. You're winding down your risk level, but while you only have a short period to retirement, you might still be living for several more decades. One of the biggest mistakes retirement-age people make is that they become too conservative with their investments, taking a short-term approach instead of planning for the long-term. They pull their money out of stocks and stock mutual funds and put it into CDs, bonds, and U.S.

Treasury Bills. Those income-bearing investments might pay decent interest rates in the short-term, but they provide no long-term appreciation. And, unlike a typical stock dividend that tends to rise with inflation, bonds and CD payments do not increase. If all of your money is in conservative investments, your buying power will be slowly eroded by inflation. You should continue to keep a good share of your assets in stocks and stock funds— maybe 30 to 60 percent, with heavier weighting going to more conservative, dividend-paying blue chips. Then keep your risks down and returns up by spreading your assets across a range of other investments, such as REITs and real estate limited partnerships (10 to 20 percent), corporate bonds (or UITs or funds), junk bond funds or UITs, mortgage-backed securities, convertible bonds, zero-coupon securities, savings bonds, STRIPS, TIPS, I-bonds, and T-bonds.

INVESTING FOR INCOME

If you don't need growth, but you do need income, your portfolio might look something like this:

25 to 50 percent stocks, heavily weighted with dividend-paying blue chip stocks and utilities (or stock mutual funds) or UITs that invest in dividend-paying stocks (those dividends will continue to climb, helping you maintain your buying power to counteract inflation); 15 to 30 percent in REITs and real estate limited partnerships; and 40 to 60 percent in a wide range of fixed-income investments, such as corporate bonds (or UITs or funds), junk bond funds or UITs, mortgage-backed securities, convertible bonds, I-bonds, T-bonds, and tax-free municipal bonds.

INVESTING FOR PRESERVATION OF CAPITAL

You're already wealthy and set for life, as long as you don't lose the money you've already accumulated. And that is a big concern. Many investors made enough in the high-tech stock market of the 1990s to be set for life. Problem was, they got greedy and kept too much of their money in the stock market instead of spreading it around. When the market tumbled, so did their portfolios. A million-dollar nest egg suddenly became a half-a-million or a quarter-million-dollar nest egg—not enough to be set for life. Once you've accumulated a solid investment nest egg sufficient to get you through retirement, why take chances? Time to trim back the riskier assets and pump up the safer ones. But you don't want to lose ground to inflation. You want to maintain your buying power without jeopardizing your fortune.

Because stocks still provide the best returns over the long term—and might pay pretty good dividends that keep moving up, keep 20 to 40 percent of your assets in a well-diversified portfolio of blue chip stocks or funds. That might seem like a high percentage, but mixed in with a number of other diverse investments, it shouldn't pose too big of a drag in a down market and could bump up your returns in a bull market. Add some REITs or real estate limited partnerships (10 to 20 percent), with the balance of your assets going into a combination of fixed-income and zero-coupon investments, such as corporate bonds (or UITs or funds), junk bond funds or UITs, mortgage-backed securities, convertible bonds, zero-coupon securities, savings bonds, STRIPS, TIPS, I-bonds, and T-bonds.

Or, if you want to keep your income taxes down, you might put 20 to 40 percent of your assets in municipal bonds. They won't provide any capital appreciation, and their yield is among the lowest of all bonds, but the interest is tax-free, and the rates tend to be somewhat higher than inflation, so you can maintain buying power.

TWEAKING YOUR PORTFOLIO

You can increase your long-term returns if you are able to make occasional adjustments in your asset mix to take advantage of changes in the economy. Here are some suggestions on how to tweak your portfolio as economic circumstances change:

- *The economy is slowing and interest rates are high*: Time to move some money out of stocks and into fixed-income investments while you can still get good yields. Put more into long-term bonds (or funds or UITs), zero-coupon bonds, and mortgage-backed securities. Interest rates tend to fall during an economic slowdown, increasing the value of existing fixed-income investments.

- *The economy is beginning to recover and interest rates are low.* Time to move some money back into stocks and commercial real estate investments, such as REITs and limited partnerships. Lighten your position in fixed-income investments, because they tend to decline in value as interest rates increase. If you need income, put some money into

TIPS (Treasury Inflation-Protected Securities) and I Bonds that increase their yield as inflation picks up. Convertible bonds might also do well now, and you might also put some money into U.S. Savings Bonds because the interest rate they pay increases as market interest rates increase. You might also want to put some money into other types of investments that do well in inflationary periods, such as oil and precious metals.

- *The economy is in full swing and interest rates are moving up.* Stocks and real estate investments are still going strong, so hold onto those investments. Oil and precious metals might be near a peak (sell the metals, hold onto the oil for a little longer). And fixed-income investments are beginning to look more appealing. Hang onto your TIPS and I Bonds, but you might want to start moving a little money into the higher-yielding fixed-income investments, such as junk bond funds, corporate bond funds, and mortgage-backed securities.

- *The economy is starting to slide, and interest rates are high.* The cycle begins again. Lower your exposure to stocks and real estate, and begin to lock in fixed-income investments at the current high rates.

Because of the uncertainty of the economy, you need to be very careful in the changes you make to your portfolio—just make small adjustments from time to time. It's impossible to anticipate with great certainty the extent of upcoming economic shifts and their impact on various assets. That's why it's important not to make radical changes in your portfolio. Hang onto your basic core components, and make minor shifts in the weighting. Or as Pope John XXIII once put it, "See everything, overlook a great deal; correct a little."

Index

Note: Boldface numbers indicate illustrations.

About the Author

Gene Walden is the best-selling author of more than 20 investment books, including *The 100 Best Stocks to Own in America.* He has been a contributor to *The Wall Street Journal, Investor's Business Daily,* and other prominent publications, and has been featured hundreds of times on CNBC, CNN, and other TV and radio programs and networks.